AF504386

For Beth,
who has been ceaselessly
by my side.

Gracias, mi amor.

I carry your heart(I carry it in my heart)

Don't forget.

And for my students. They blessed me with a profoundly meaningful gift – the opportunity to witness and play a part in the blossoming of the creative spirit.

One looks back with appreciation to the brilliant teachers, but with gratitude to those who touched our human feelings. The curriculum is so much necessary raw material, but warmth is the vital element for the growing plant and for the soul of the child.

\- Carl Jung

There are any number of people to whom I owe an immense debt of gratitude for helping me in my path to success in the classroom, but at the top of the list are Frank Ratliff, Ron Cooper, Deanna Messinger, Sharon Ferguson, Leslie Goldman, and Robin Levy. All of them were master teachers who inspired me with their example, their faith in me, and their incredible kindness as I made my way down this path.

A portion of the proceeds from this book will be donated to the ongoing effort to find a cure for ALS.

Is It OK To Eat Expired Macarons?
Observations and Conversations From a
Middle School Art Classroom

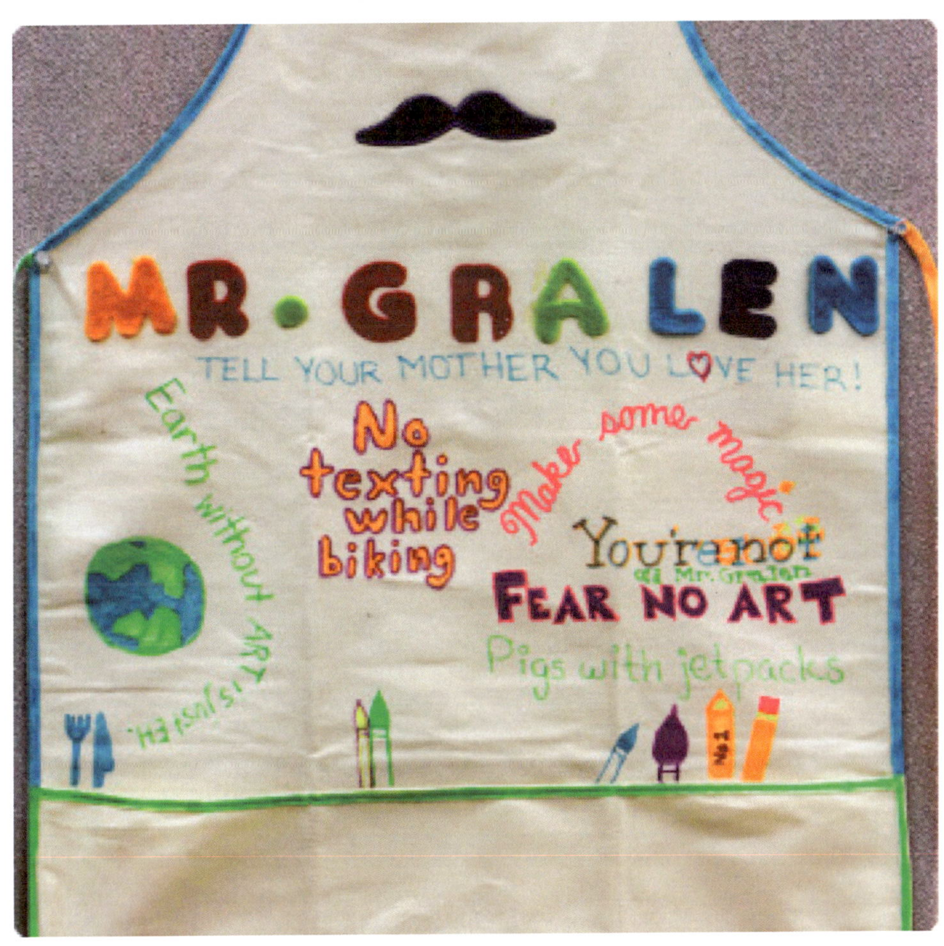

A couple of kids made this apron for me just before the winter break one year. It had all my favorite "trademark" sayings on it.

It made me cry.

I was a middle school art teacher for twenty years and I got to work with some amazing kids. They kept me young at heart and honest, and they enriched my soul and life in ways that were unimaginable to me before I started teaching.

Middle school is a peculiar time in a kid's life. My own memories of middle school are mixed and tumultuous. Kids are just finding out who they are and are doing all sorts of experimenting with their identities. They are often still "innocent" enough to be themselves, just before the pernicious filters of ego and self-consciousness can shut down the magic and joy of creative expression.

Every day my students provided endlessly fascinating, humorous, and touching moments. I consider myself a lucky man that I got to witness this magic on a daily basis. And they did create some gloriously expressive art…

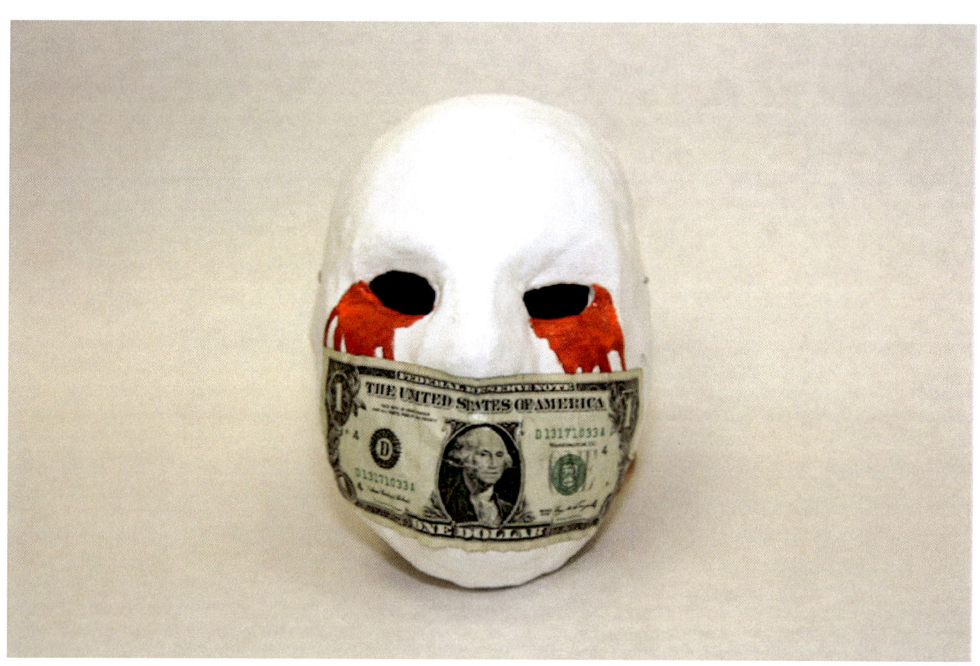

I had a very thoughtful 8th-grade girl in my class who was quite upset about what was happening during the Occupy Wall Street protests in 2008. She wanted her mask to reflect her concerns.

I asked her what she thought was going on. She paused, and said, "People are being silenced by money." I reached into my wallet and gave her a dollar, and said "How can you use that to show what you feel?" When I returned to her table, this is what she had done.…

And they said the funniest things. So over the years I took some notes….

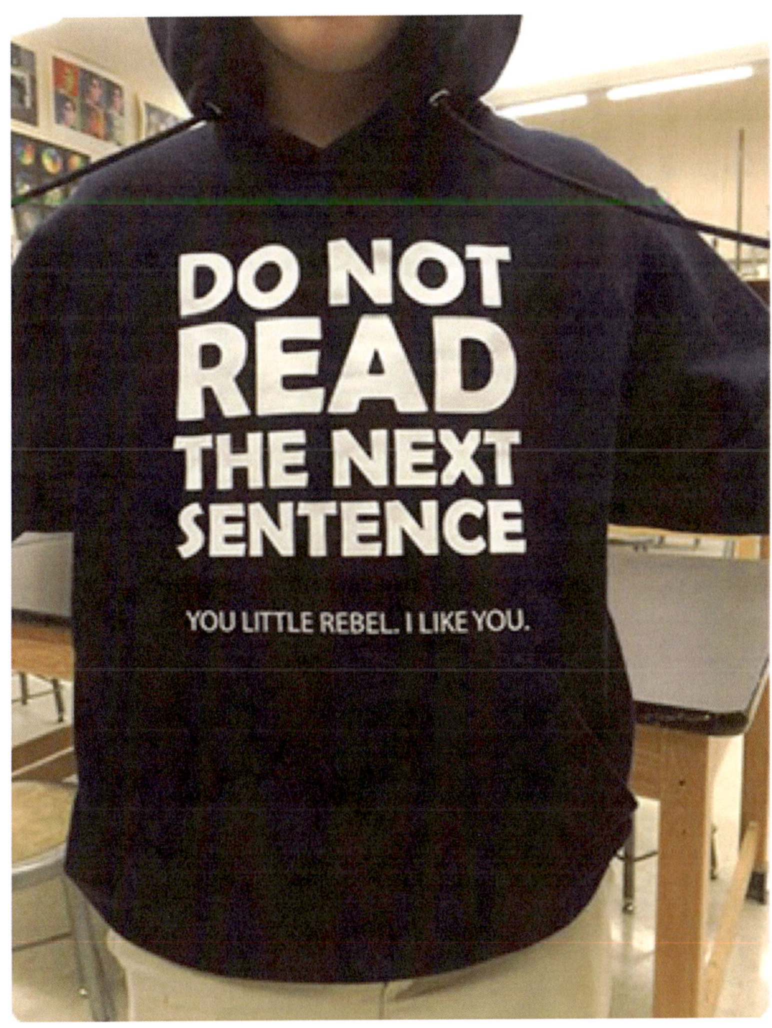

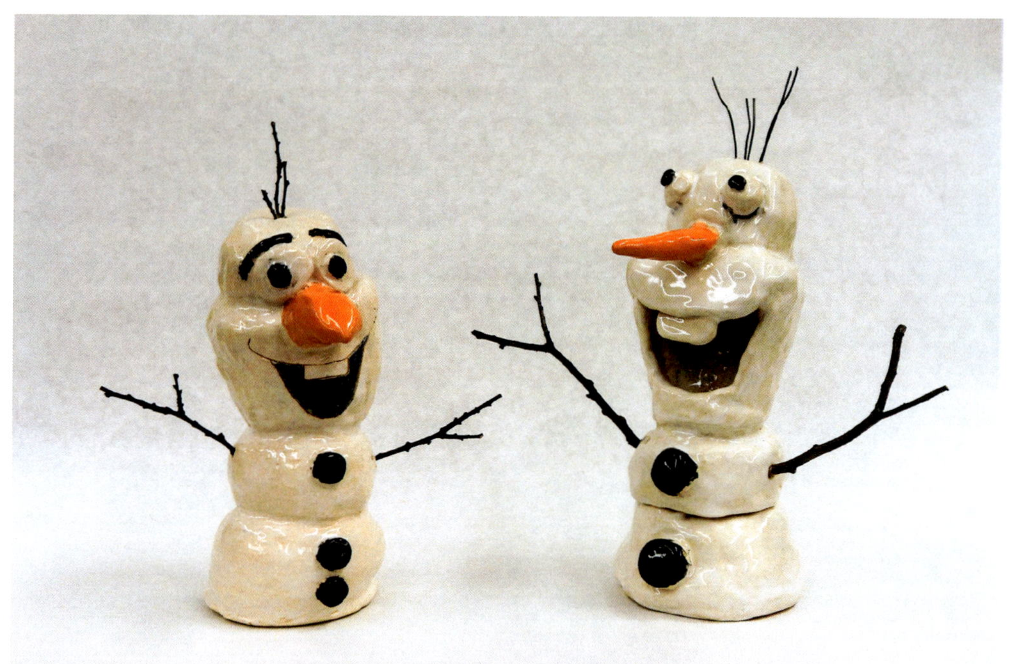

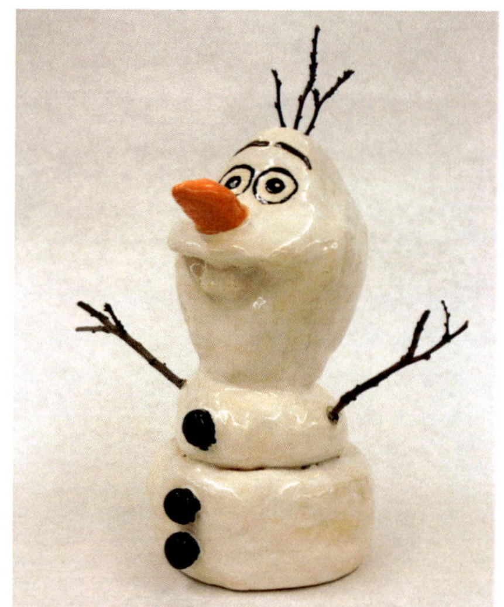

Me: Why don't you put a pair of rainbow-colored wings on Mike Pence?

Kid: Who's Mike Pence?

Kid: Know what I do with my art when I take it home?

Me: Give it to your mom?

Kid: Nope. I sell it to my dad.

I'm playing "Winter Wonderland" on Spotify:

Me: Do you guys know who Bing Crosby is?

Kid: Wait, this is Bill Cosby?

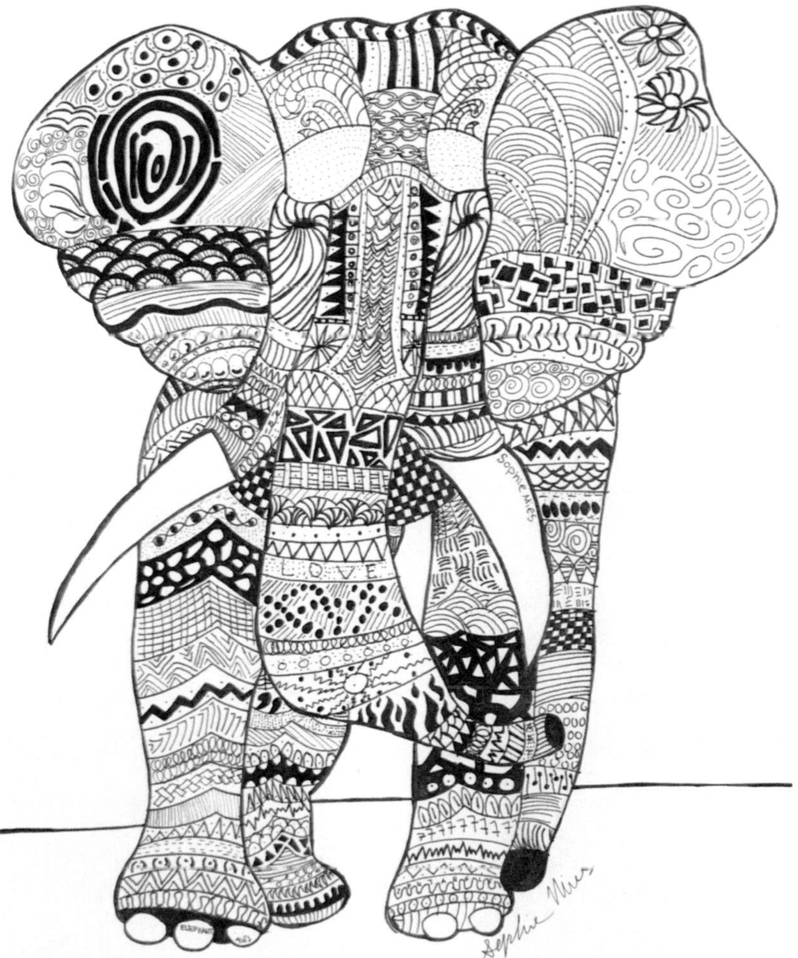

I overhear some kids talking about their plans for next summer, which includes getting a first job:

Me: You're getting a job? Where?

Kid: On an island off the coast of Boston. It's called Martha's Vineyard. Have you heard of it?

Me: When are you gonna be done with this?

Kid: Two more days?

Me: I want you to finish it so that I can put it in the art show. Does that motivate you?

Kid: My motivation comes from the inside.

Me: Remember – becoming a decent human being is an ongoing project, something that takes work and attention every day.

Kid: I'm really bad at long-term projects.

7

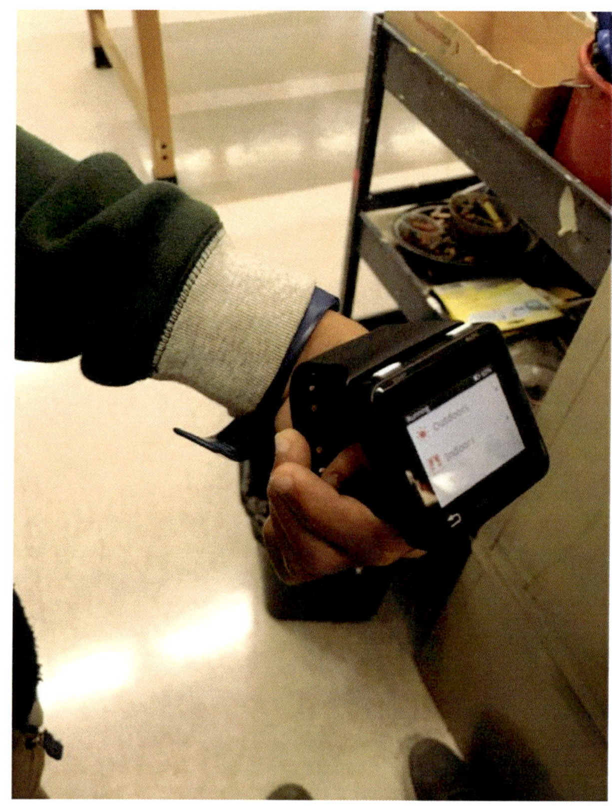

Well before the Apple Watch, a kid came into the room and showed me this enormous wrist computing device:

Kid: Check this out, Mr. Gralen. My dad wrote the code for this before I was born. It's ancient. I could probably sell it on eBay for two thousand dollars.

On the morning of the day they decided to close the schools because of the covid pandemic, I decide to show a movie because the kids know that school is closed and they're all acting more insane than they usually are. So I show them a movie, and they are jabbering and talking over the show. I stop the movie and lecture them sternly:

Me: You are not at home, sitting on the couch, watching Netflix. You are in a shared environment with twenty-three other people, and you need to behave appropriately.

Kid: I feel like I'm at home – I get yelled at there, too.

Kid #1: *summarily handing me a scrap piece of clay* Mr. G., can you deal with this, please?

Me: What do I look like, a butler?

Kid #1: Well, yeah, you sort of do.

Kid #2: It's the mustache.

Overheard:

Kid: My brother, who is 16 years old, has spent over $100 on Fortnite. I hate that I have the same genes as that guy.

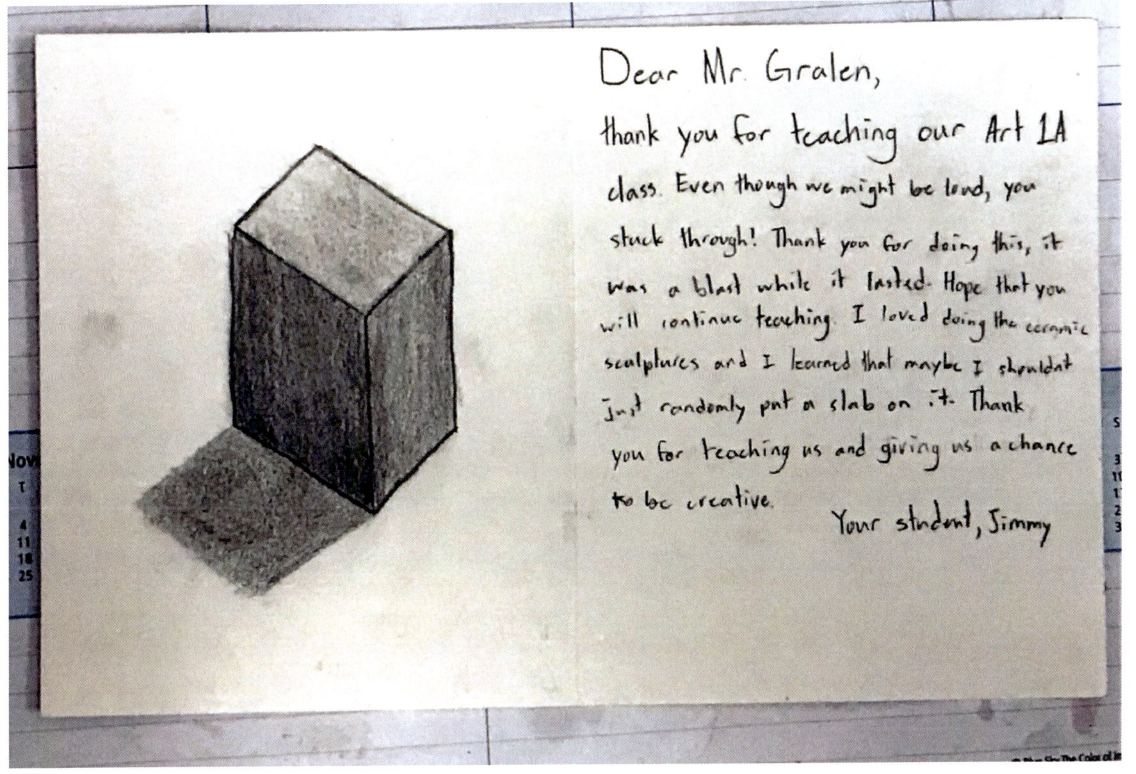

This was a very rambunctious class. I love "Hope that you will continue teaching", as if that was questionable after their class...

We had an interesting discussion this morning about laundry:

Kid: I wash my sheets every two days.

Me: Well, do you wash them or does your mom wash them?

Kid: We have people.

Overheard (and one of those things you really don't want to think about too much….):

Kid: There is something supernatural going on in the boy's locker room right now.

Kid: I got bored with this part of the drawing.

Me: You got bored? Oh no, what are we gonna do about that?

Kid: Draw dead people?

There are three weeks left in the school year. Promise me you will use them wisely. Make lots of art, be safe, do good work, tell your parents you love them. Here's a picture of a baby sloth.

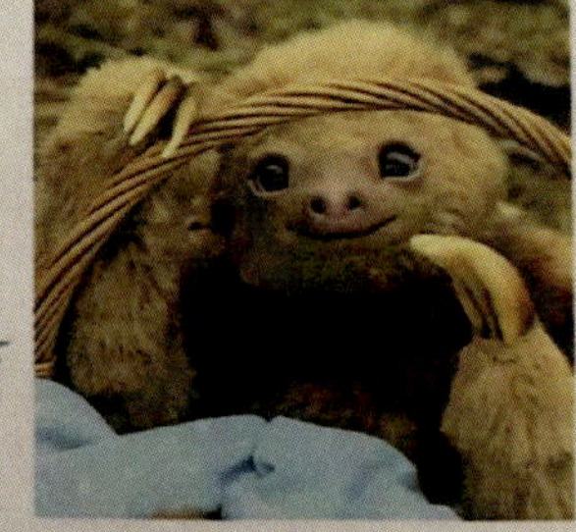

Thank you for being such a wonderful teacher this year, and for pushing me to do difficult things I didn't want to.

Write your paragraph here:

My mask is Batman. I used a smooth, matte texture to show similarity to Batman's real mask. I mixed black and clear, glitter paint colors together to make it more unique and also because glitter. The masks represents that I like Batman, and that I am a controlling person who likes everything my way, and so does Batman. Additionally, he's rich, hot, and cool.

Kid: Mr. G., what was the first job you ever had?

Me: Delivering prescriptions for the local pharmacy on my bicycle, when I was your age.

Kid: So you were a drug dealer when you were 12?

Overheard at lunch:

Kid #1: Did you know that a yawn is just a slow-motion sneeze?

Kid #2: But without the snot.

Time of the Trump Presidency:

Me: You can share these supplies. Sharing is a good character trait to develop at your age, so we're going to keep working on that, even though you aren't getting good role modeling on it from some adults in our society.

Kid: Why do you keep saying that?

5. Here is a picture of a kitten. How does this make you feel?

That just made my day

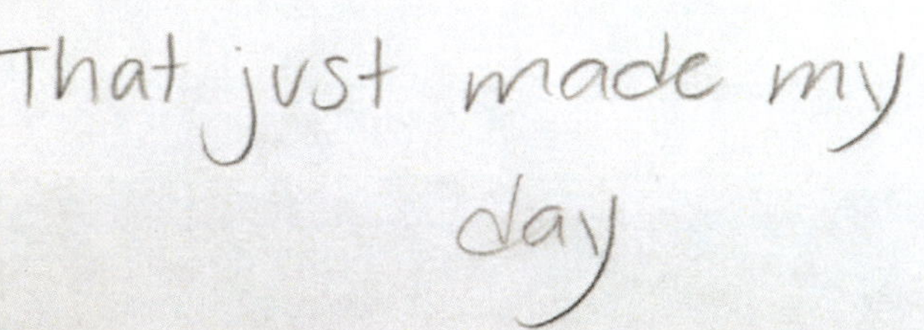
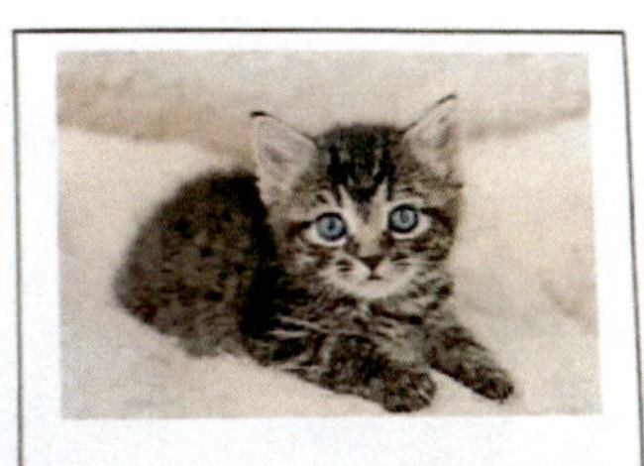

5. Here is a picture of a kitten. How does this make you feel?

It makes me feel like I need a cat, But it would probably eat my birds.

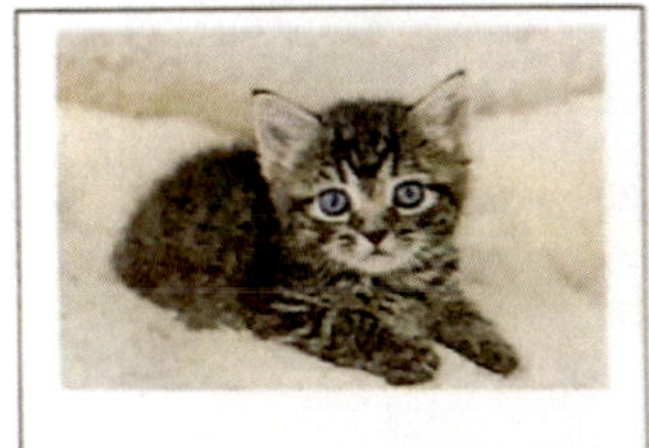

5. Here is a picture of a kitten. How does this make you feel?

Its staring into my soul and judging me for my sins. Also I'm allergic to cats.

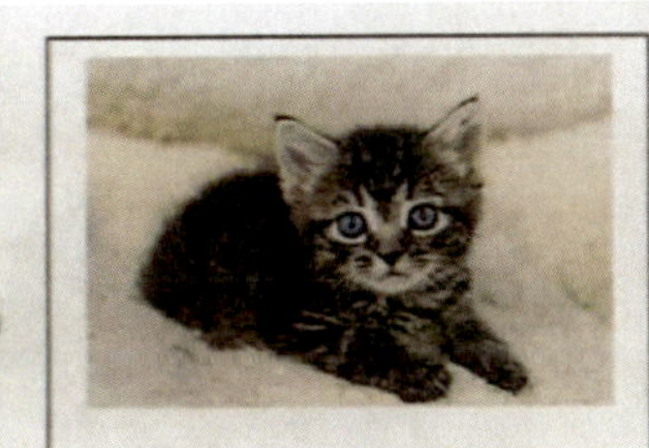

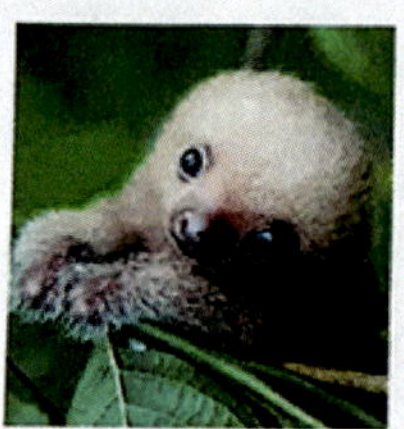

Say hello to this baby sloth and tell me how it makes you feel.

Kid: Mr. G., why do we have quizzes? They just check to see how good we did on our work during the week, after we already finished all of it already.

Me: Well I'm guessing your grammar quiz might not have had the best results.

Me: What's wrong, kiddo?

Kid: Nothing.

Me: You're walking around like a zombie.

Kid: That doesn't necessarily mean that anything's wrong.

Kid: You're making me feel guilty, Mr. G.

Me: I'll do anything that works. And I'm pretty good at using that tactic, since I was raised Catholic. The Catholics are really good at inducing guilt.

Kid: I'll bet they're nowhere near as good as my Chinese parents.

Me: Good morning, my beloved precious identically unique flameproof snowflakes.

Kid: Not applicable to me, Mr. G. I'm feeling pretty flammable today.

Me: I'm gonna play you guys some '80s music.

Kid: I get enough of that from my parents.

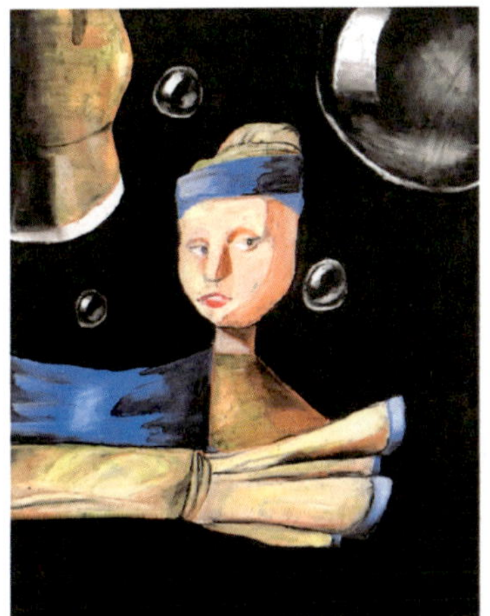
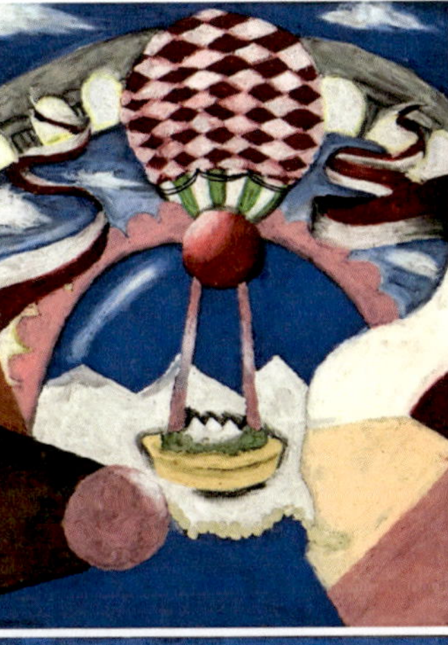
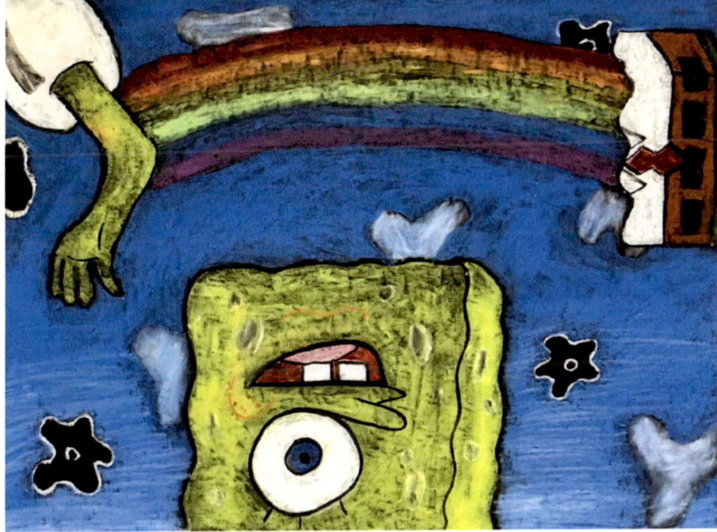

ABSTRACT DRAWING IN OIL PASTEL

I love it that the spectrum on this project runs from Vermeer to SpongeBob.

Kids are lit this morning:

Me: You should definitely not be watching "Deadpool 2." It is totally inappropriate for you.

Kid: What about "50 Shades of Grey?"

Me: Do you know who Mr. Rogers was?

Kid: Wasn't he a rabbit?

Me: You should stop using TikTok. They're stealing your data every time you log on.

Kid: But I have unlimited data from AT&T.

13

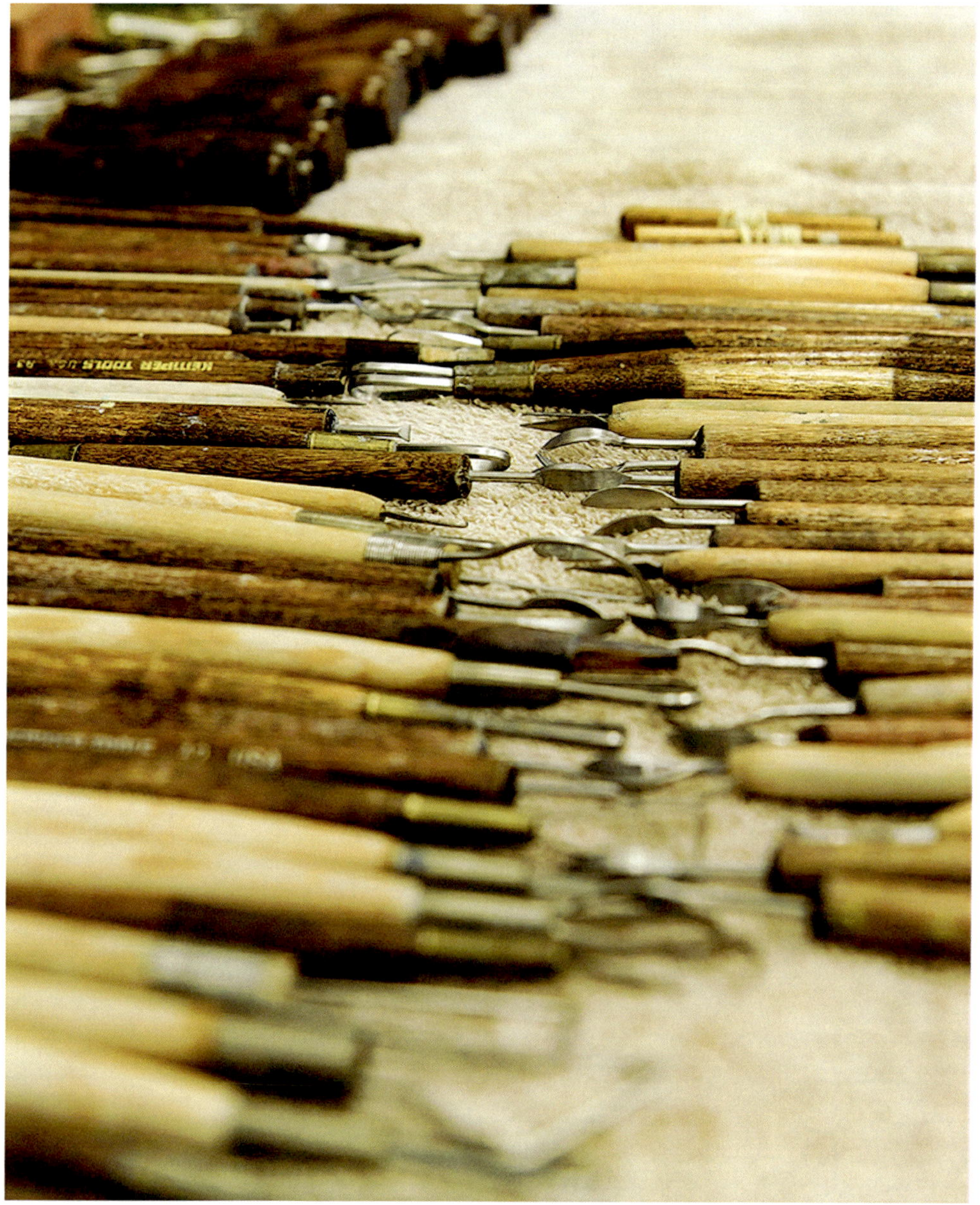

First day of school…

Kid: How old are you?

Me: How old do you think I am?

Kid: How old do you feel?

And so it begins…

Me: That game, Fortnite? It will eventually die, just like Vine and fidget spinners.

Kid: Have you ever really thought about the eventual heat death of the universe, Mr. G.?

Me: That escalated quickly.

Kid: Mr. G., can you play something a little more interesting?

Me: Jeez, you are impossible to please.

Kid: I'm very pleased when people do what I say.

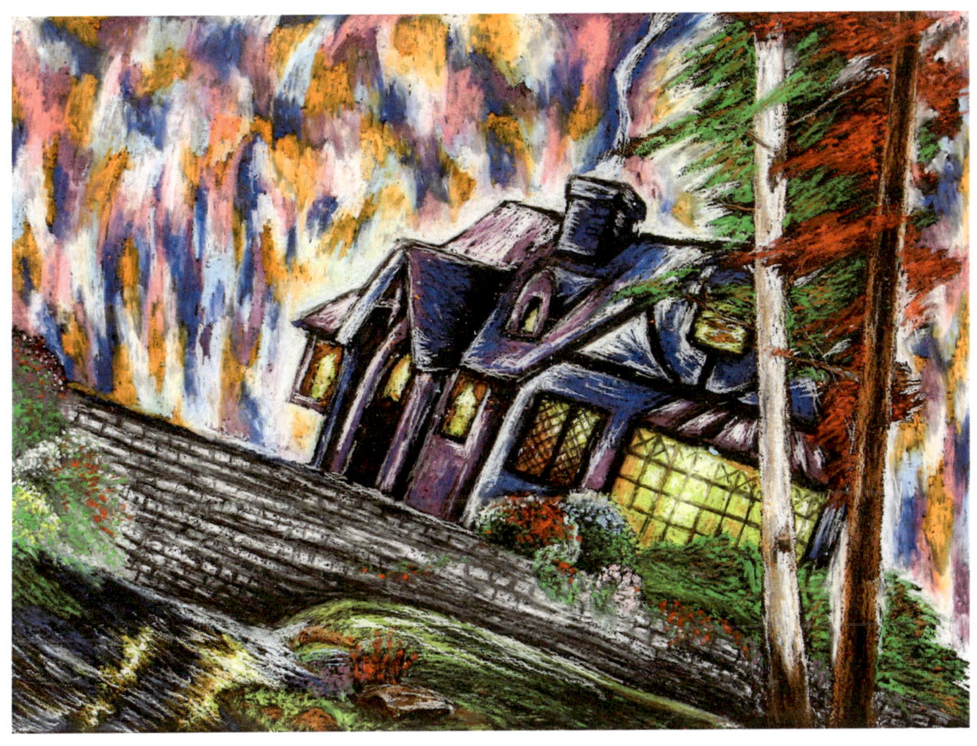

One of my very best students chose a Thomas Kinkade painting as the source image for her abstract drawing. Kinkade, a true master of kitsch, is most definitely NOT on my list of favorite painters, but I restrained myself from saying anything.

Then she drew it like it was on fire and sinking.

Love that kid.

Me: Is it ever too early to eat pickles?

Kid #1: Well, at some point it's always too early, because then it's a cucumber.

Kid #2: Wait, whaaat? Pickles are cucumbers?

Me: OK, you need to quit messing around and get to work.

Kid: I don't wanna do this.

Me: You're acting like a 3-year old.

Kid: I identify as a 3-year old.

Three kids are having a very interesting discussion about kindness and honesty:

Kid #1: You should always temper your honesty with kindness.

Kid #2: Being kind comes naturally if you have love in your heart.

Kid #3: Politeness is just pre-packaged deceit.

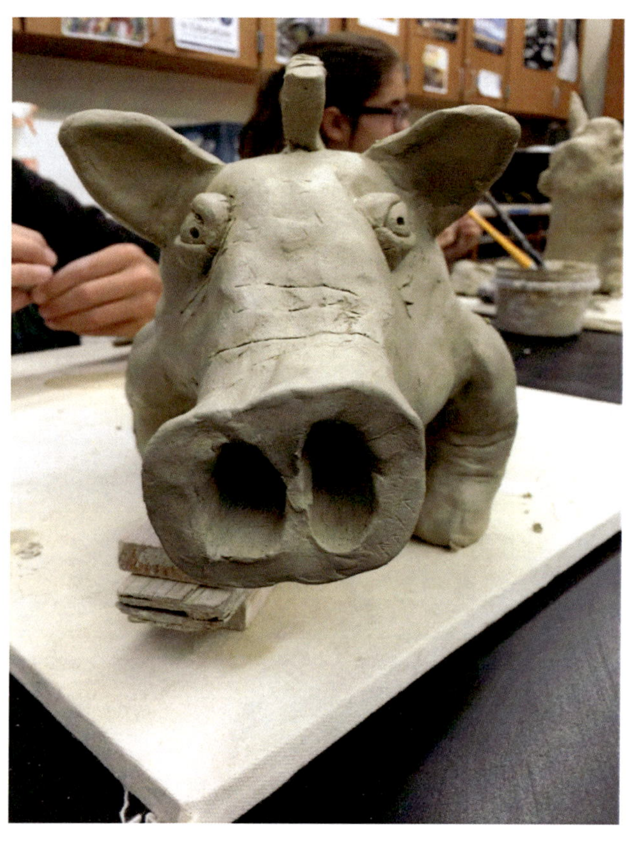

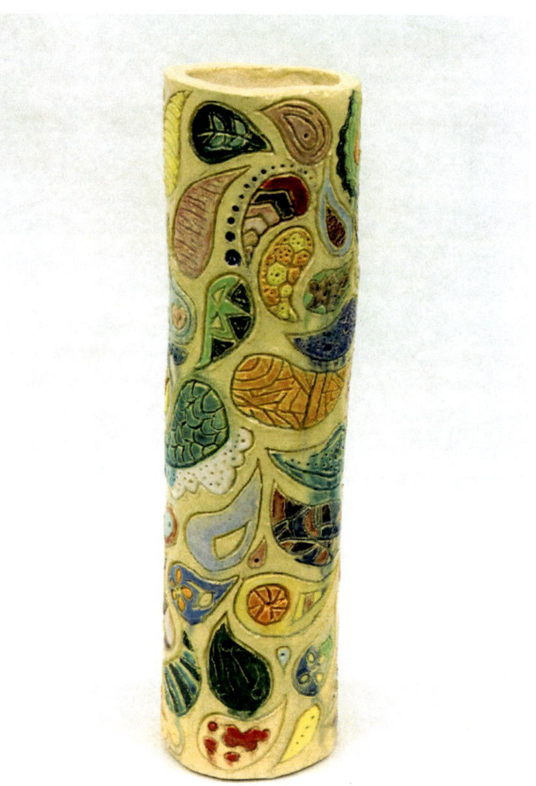

Kid #1: How old are you?

Me: How old do you think I am?

Kid #1: That depends. Do you want flattery or honesty?

Kid #2: No, how old are you, really?

Me: Let's turn this into a math problem.

Kid #2: Why would you do that?

Me: I was born in 1960. Do the math.

Kid #2: *long pause*. YOU'RE EIGHTY?

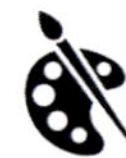

Kid is looking sad:

Me: What's wrong?

Kid: I don't know, Mr. G.,the world is a weird place. Like, sometimes Twitter is just a giant pile of hate fire.

I'm working with a big piece of pottery and I need some help. I turn to a kid:

Me: Can you do me a favor?

Kid: That depends. I'm not gonna bury a body.

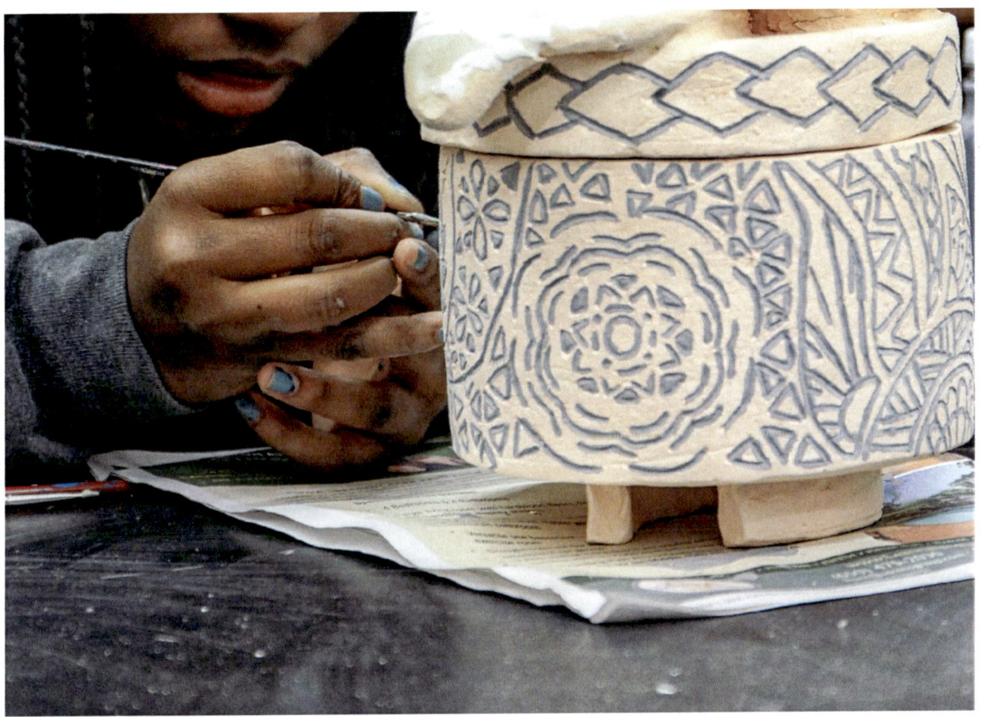

Kid: I don't like doing this, Mr. G.

Me: I don't like paying my taxes every year, but I do because there are some things you just have to follow through on.

Kid: I'm going to have my mom do my taxes when I grow up.

Me: You're going to have your mom do your taxes for the rest of your life?

Kid: When she dies, I'll make my husband do it.

Me: This one is going to be a little more challenging for you, and that's a good thing.

Kid: I don't wanna do this.

Me: You're whining like a 5-year old.

Kid: I'm fine with that.

Kid #1: Mr. G., how old are you?

Me: I'm 58. Is that old?

Kid #1: Well, yeah, it is. I mean it's old to us, but it's not really old. But yeah, it's old.

Kid #2: You should just stop talking.

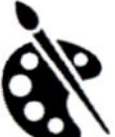

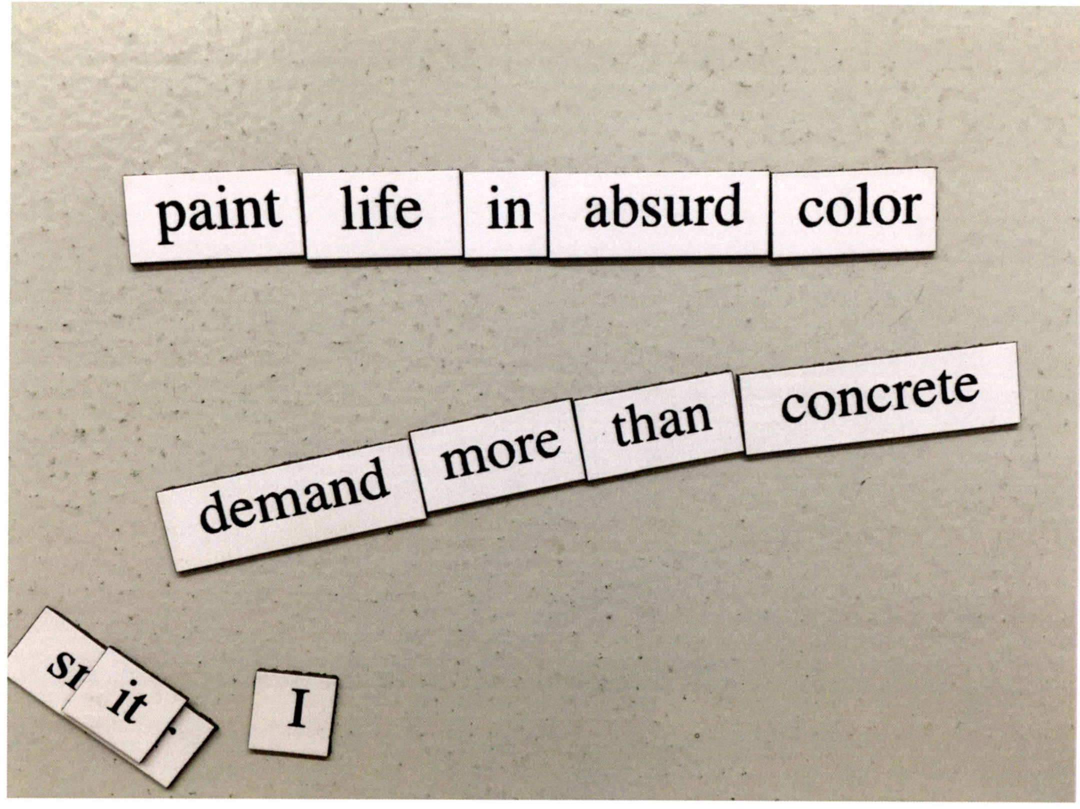

Kid #1: Let's go have snacks in the on-call room.

Kid #2: Actually, the on-call room is for sex.

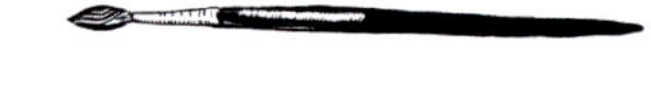

Kid #1: My friend went to a farm in Vermont and she got traumatized when they cut the head off a chicken and it ran around the yard.

Kid #2: Did you know that a woman can give birth to a baby after she's dead?

Kid #3: I know, I saw that on Grey's Anatomy.

Kid #4: Did you know that men can get erections after they die?

Me: Thanks for sharing.

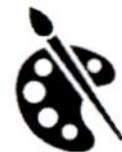

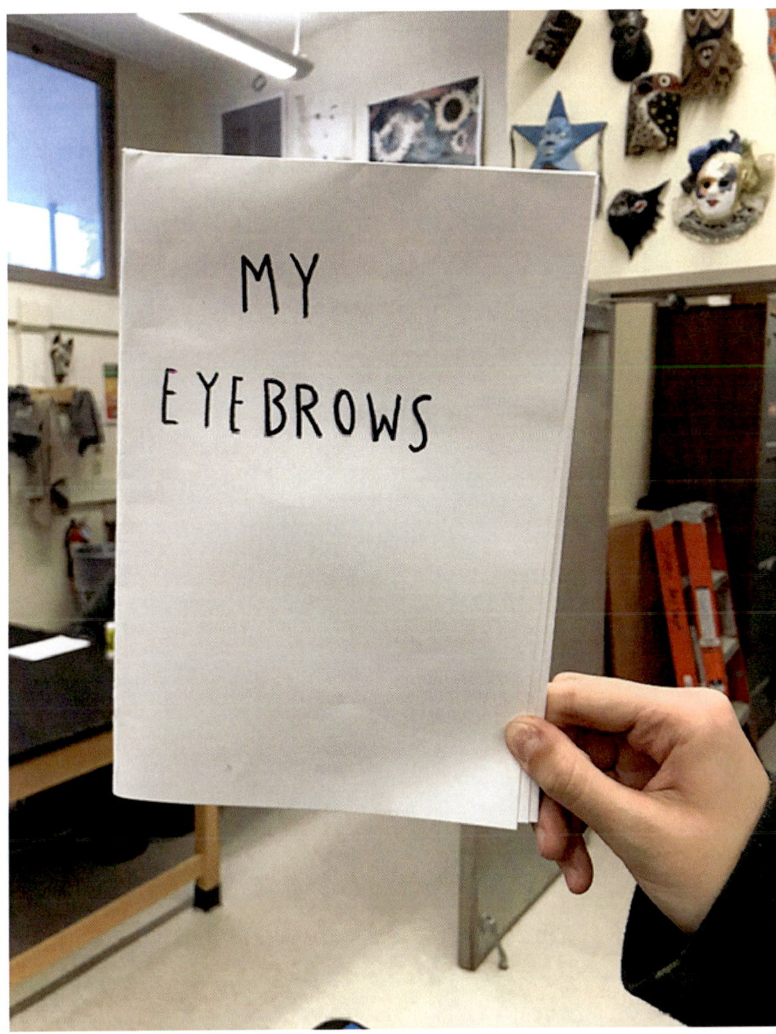

"Your book can be on any topic that you are passionate about…"

Me: OK, you guys, I'm gonna spice things up for you this morning and play some Vivaldi.

Kid: Oh no! That's some composer guy, isn't it?

Kids are singing "Summer Loving" from "Grease":

Kid #1: That Frank Sinatra guy could really sing, but he wasn't a very good actor.

Kid #2: You mean John Travolta.

Kid #3: My mom is from the '80s and she listens to that Sinatra guy all the time.

Girl: This is really hard for me today because I have a syndrome.

Boy: Wait, what syndrome do you have?

Girl: Pre-menstrual? [rolls eyes]

Boy: Is that a thing?

Girl sees me trying really hard not to laugh: "Mr. G., this is really hard. I literally had hysterics last night when my mom served rice for dinner. I DIDN'T WANT RICE."

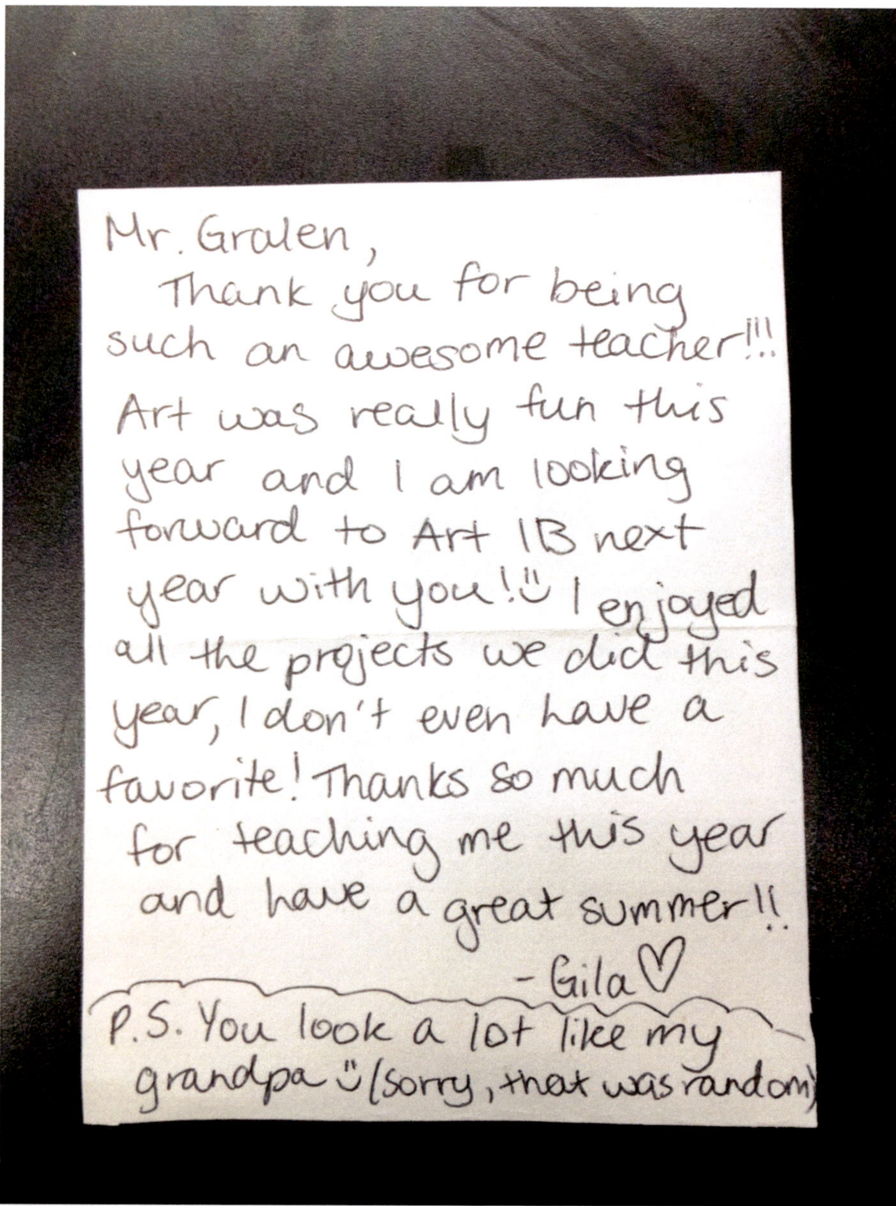

Me: Your drawing is due today.

Kid: It's not ready yet.

Me: Tell the truth, you just didn't do it, right?

Kid: I can neither confirm nor deny that.

Me: I think my iPod died this morning, you guys.

Kid: What's an iPod?

Kid #1: Mr. G., I think I'm done.

Kid #2: There's always room for improvement!

Kid #1: Mr. G., can you come over here and improve this for me?

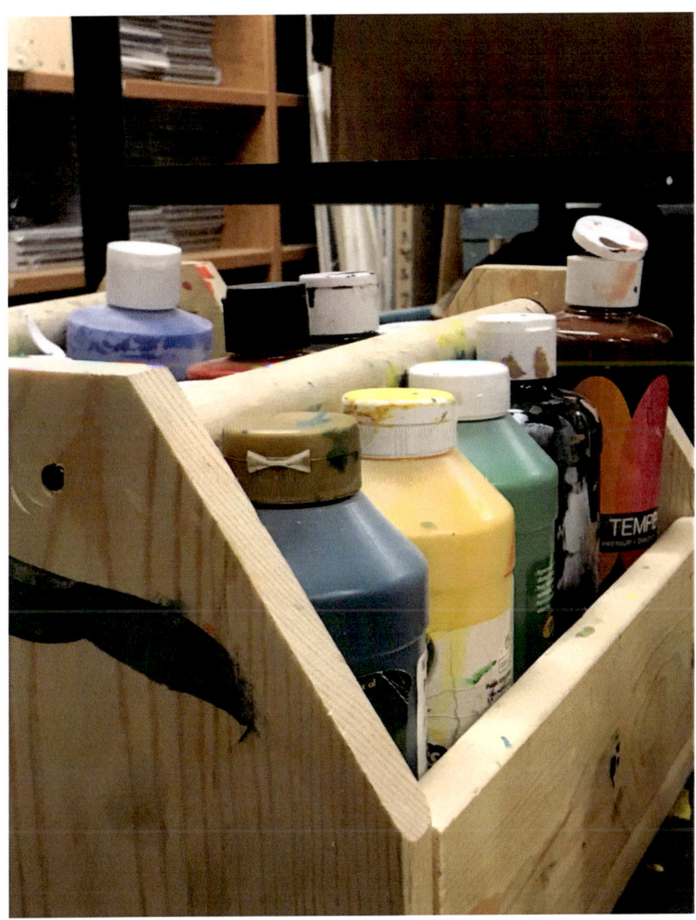

Bonus question at the bottom of the self-reflection form: "If you were a teacher and the kids in your class would not listen to you, what would you do?":

Kid: I would know that I would need to present myself with more authority.

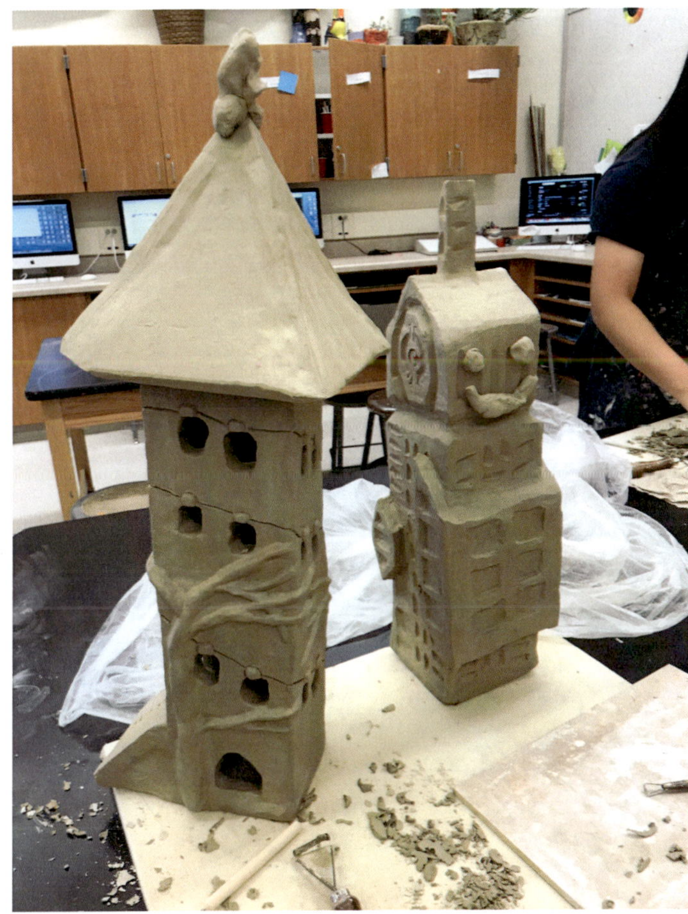

I'm showing the end of the period video of my favorite YouTube baker, Yolanda, making a Nutella Mega-Cake. At the end she is sorting hazelnuts to decorate:

Yolanda: Only the most perfect hazelnuts are chosen to decorate the top of the cake.

Kid: That's bakery eugenics.

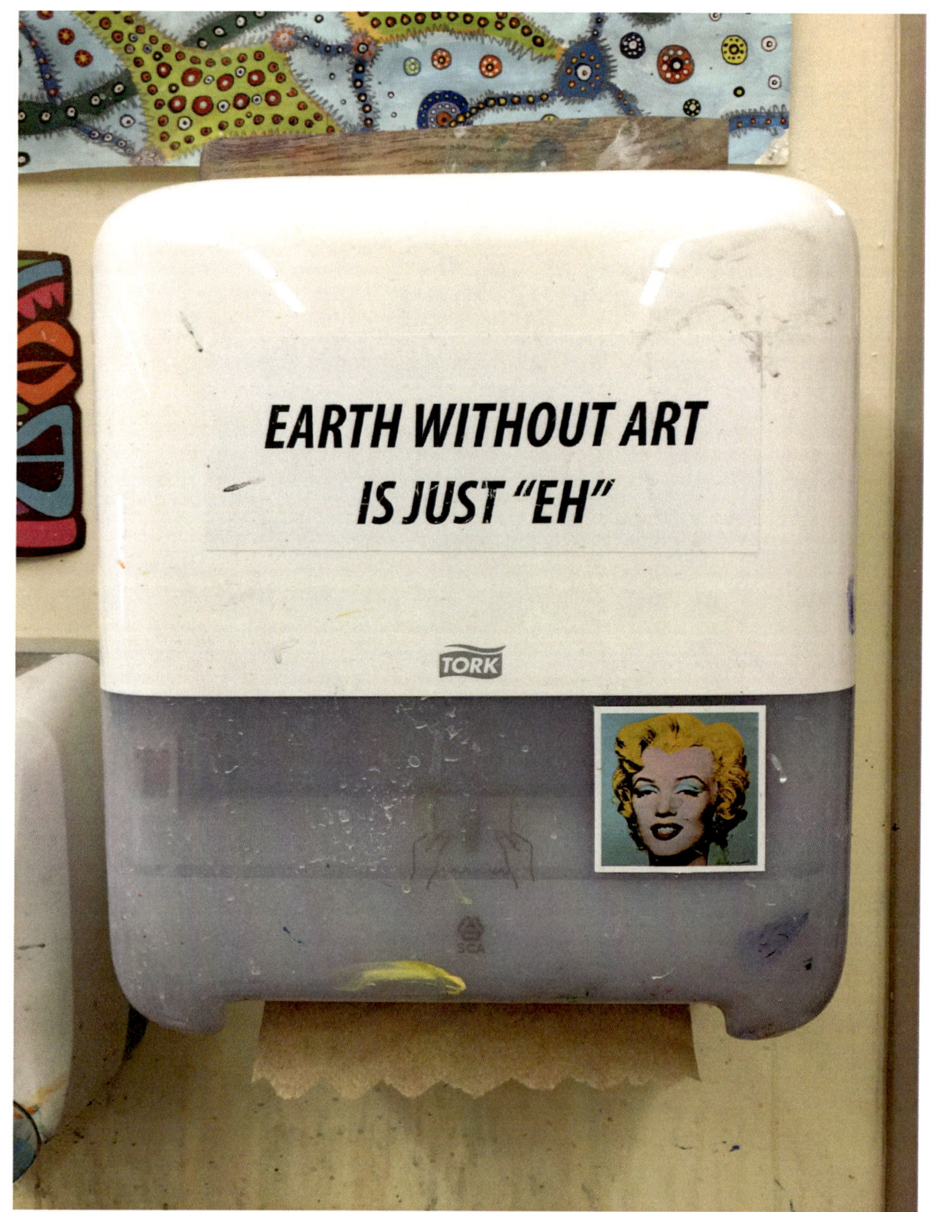

I was complimenting our band students for doing a concert this morning for some elementary school kids:

Me: Good for you! Showing kindness toward small children is good for your soul.

Kid: What if you don't like small children?

Kid #1: Mr. G., I'm afraid this drawing is not going to work.

Me: The only thing you have to fear is fear itself.

Kid #2: And bears.

Kid #1: What is the difference between hair and fur?

Kid #2: They're the same thing.

Kid #1: So I have split ends in my fur.

Me: Middle schoolers are so good at finding a reason to do the exact opposite of what you're telling them to do.

Kid: It's called "having an authority problem," Mr. G.

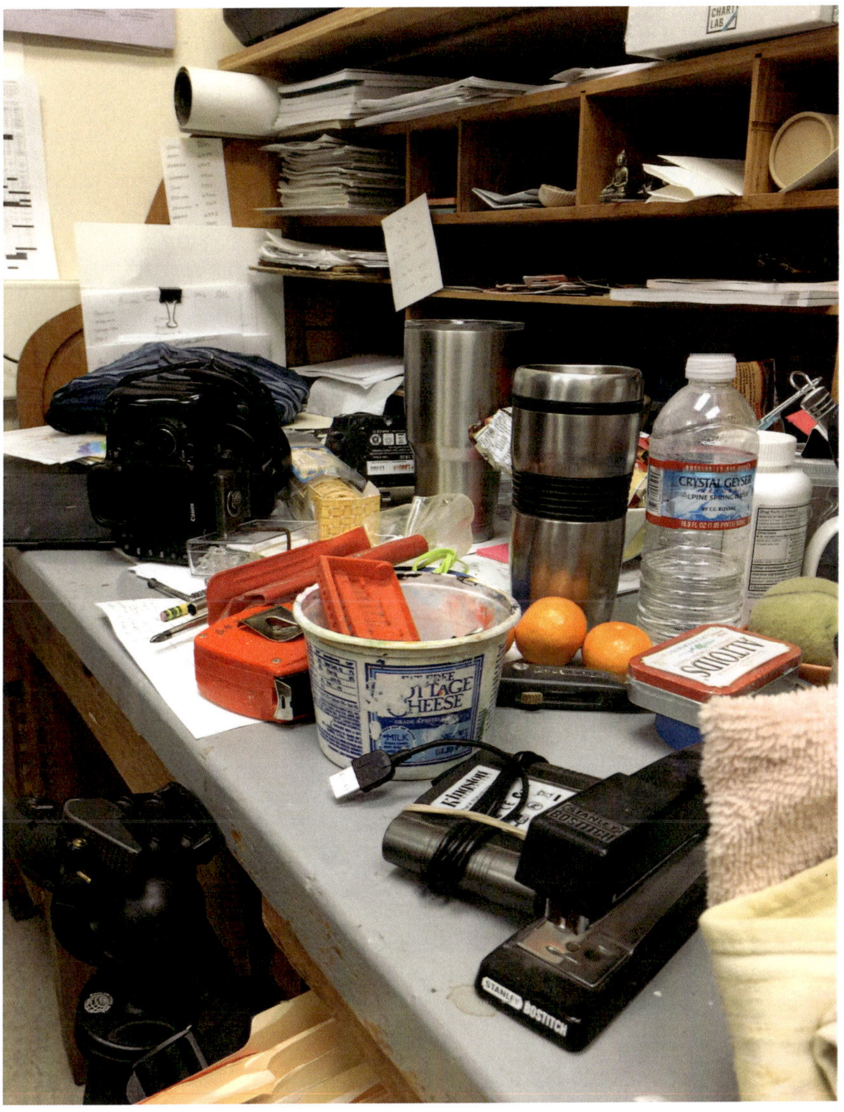

The Art Teacher's Desk

Kid who's had multiple behavior issues around his computer use limps into class on crutches this morning:

Me: What happened to you?

Kid: I dropped my Chromebook on my foot.

Me: Years from now, when you're sitting around the campfire with your grandchildren, you can tell them about actually making things with your own hands, before the robots took over.

Kid: But it will be an electric campfire, Mr. G.

Kid: What are you taking pictures of, Mr. G?

Me: Sculptures.

Kid: We're all sculptures. We were sculpted by our moms.

Me: To be fair, your dad had something to do with it too.

Kid: You had to go there, didn't you?

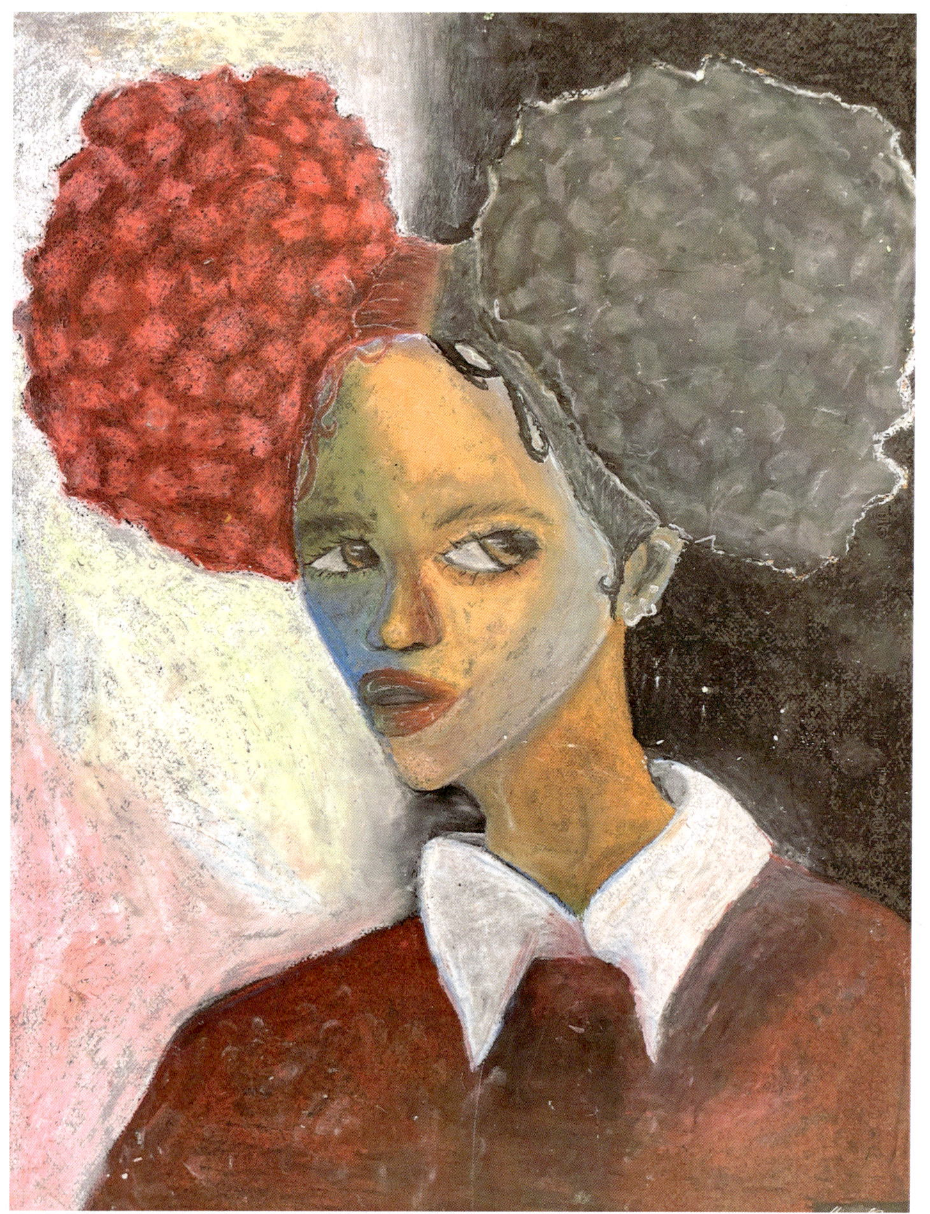

Kid #1: Siri gets pissed at you if you ask her too many questions.

Kid #2: Like "Do you have a soul?"

Kid: Mr. Gralen, do you have children?

Me: No, I don't have any kids.

Kid: You should adopt some.

Me: I think I might be a little too old to adopt.

Kid: Weren't the people who adopted Ann of Green Gables really old?

We are having a drawing contest in the classroom:

Kid: Mr. Gralen, if I pay you $10, will you make me the winner?

Me: I hate to break it to you, but if you're talking about trying to bribe me, you can't afford me.

Kid: I could take out a loan.

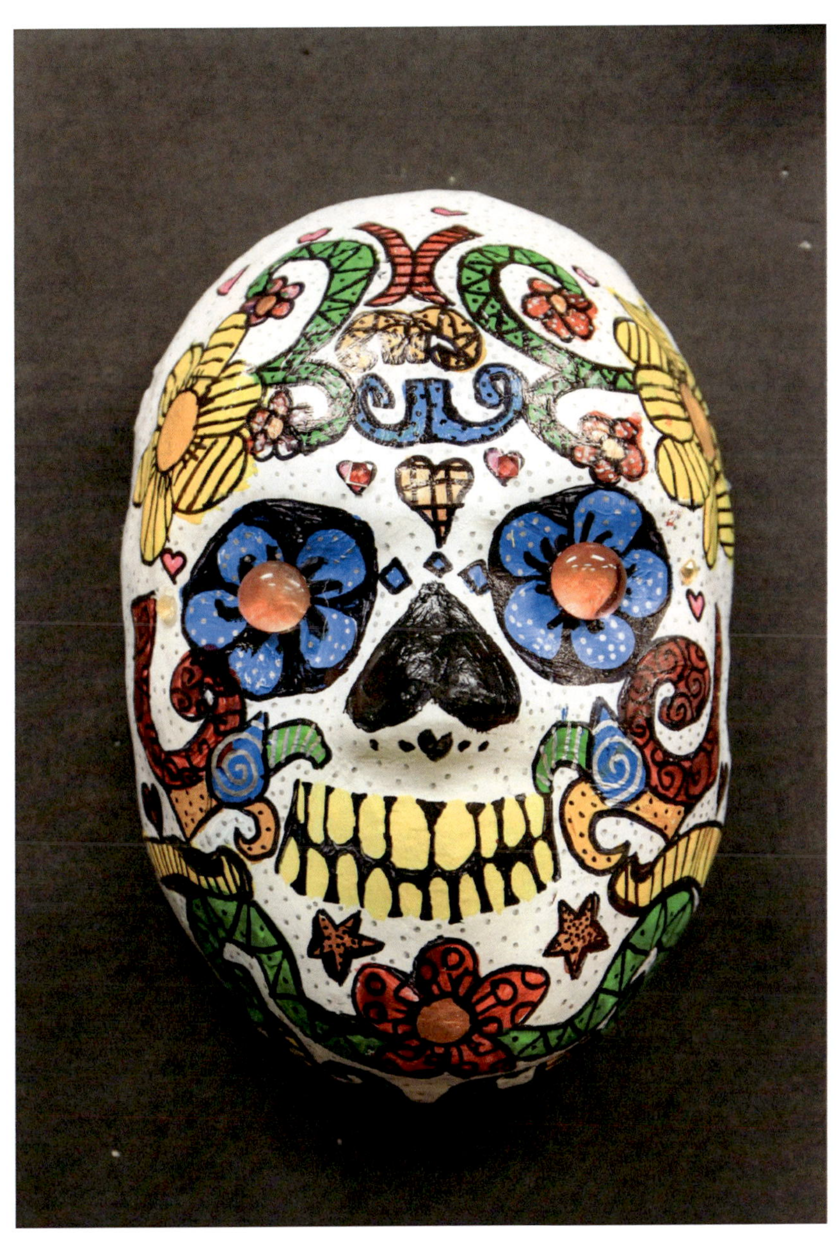

Me: I'm tired. It's been a long week.

Kid: You say that at the end of every week.

Me: I spent the weekend taking care of a 3-month old baby. It was fun.

Kid: I hate little kids. They're basically just poop and vomit machines.

Kid #1: Mr. G, did you major in art in college?

Me: No, I double-majored in Philosophy and Theatre.

Kid #2: Isn't philosophy really boring?

Kid #1: NO! Knowledge is knowing the tomato is a fruit. Wisdom is not putting that fruit into a fruit salad. Philosophy is wondering whether ketchup is a smoothie.

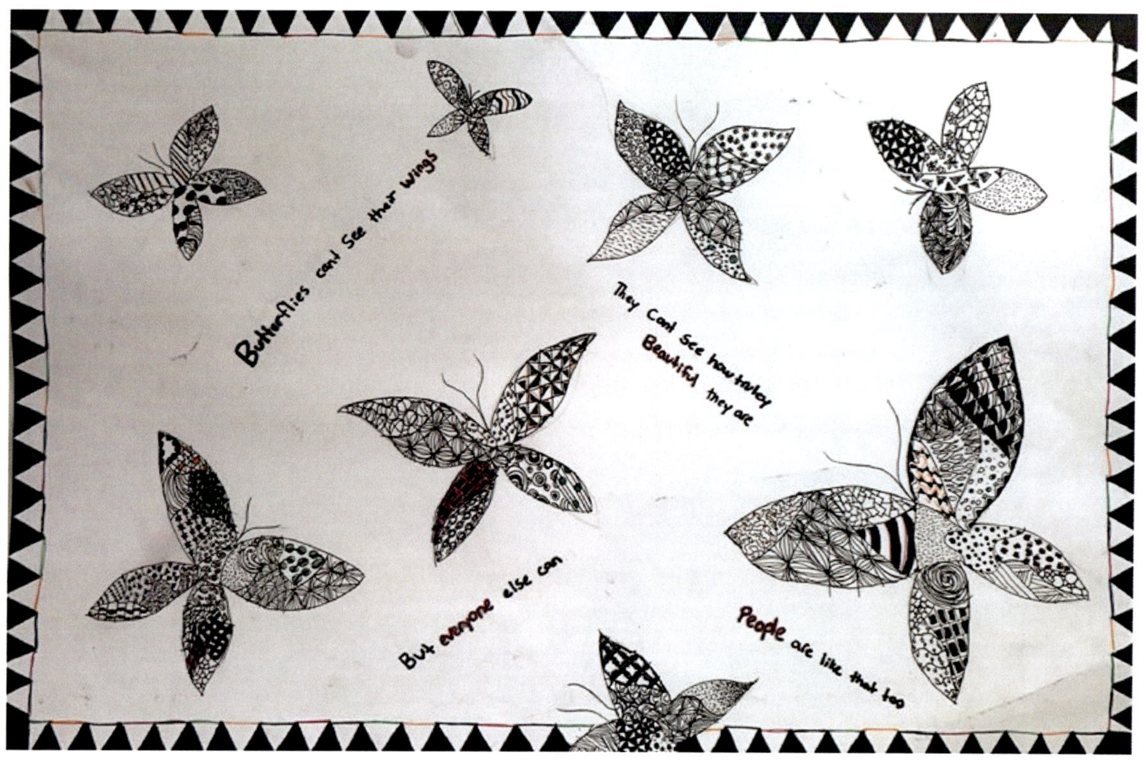

Me: What should I get my wife for her birthday?

Kid #1: Get her a vacuum cleaner.

Kid #2: Wrong. You never get her something that plugs in for her birthday.

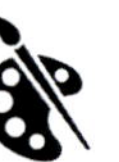

Me: The answer to that question is, "Yes, Mr. Gralen, we always want to improve our skills."

Kid #1: I like how you answer your own questions.

Me: I call it the unitary Socratic method.

Kid #1: Wasn't he one of those guys, what are they called?

Kid #2: Philosophers.

Kid #1: Wait a minute, I thought this was Ceramics class?

Butterflies can't see their wings.
They can't see how beautiful they are,
But everyone else can.
People are like that too.

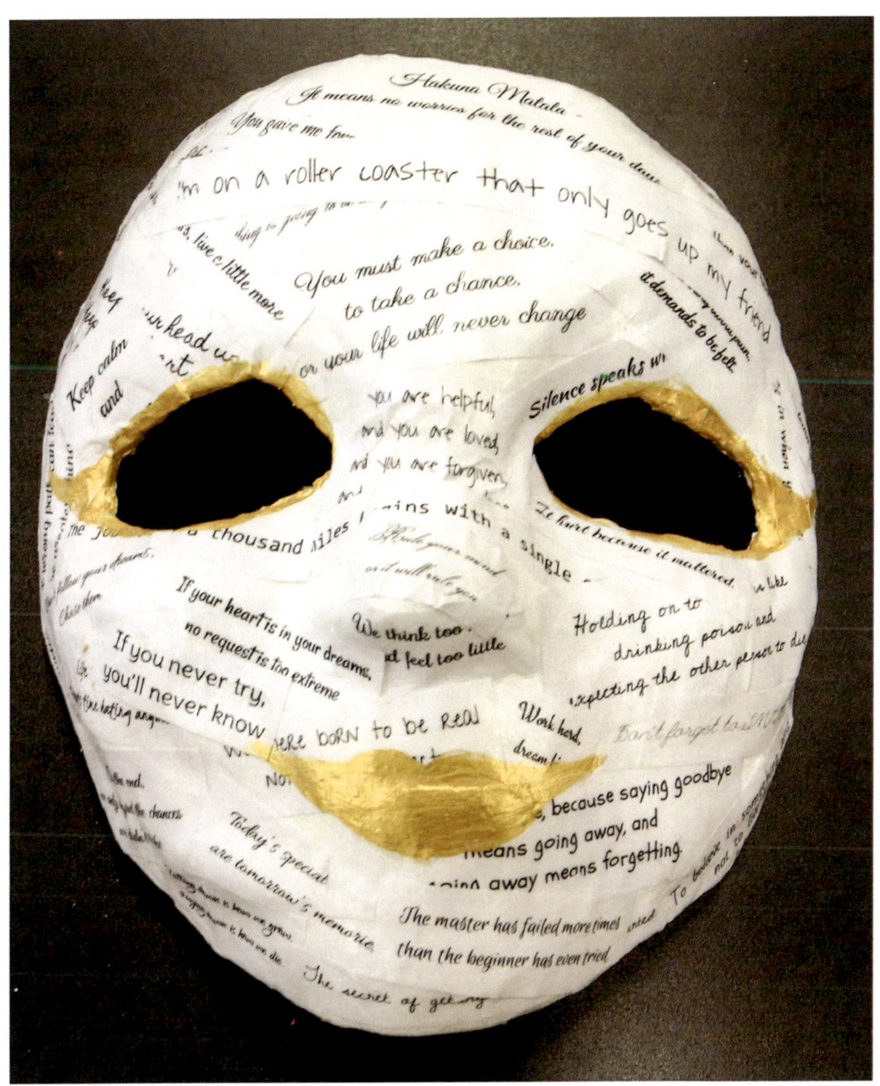

I'm on a roller coaster that only goes up, my friend.

Me: One day you will look back and remember the stories I told you about what life was like before the robots took over.

Kid taps Apple Watch and asks Siri: What's it like to be Queen?

Siri: I can't answer that right now.

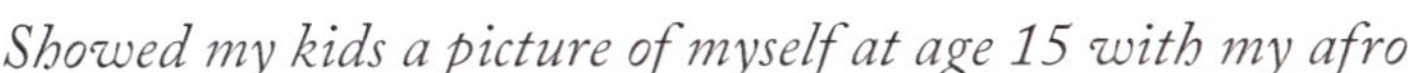

Showed my kids a picture of myself at age 15 with my afro:

Kid #1: I thought that was Bob Ross.

Kid #2: You look like an adult Ron Weasley.

Kid #3: *looks at pic, looks at me* What happened?

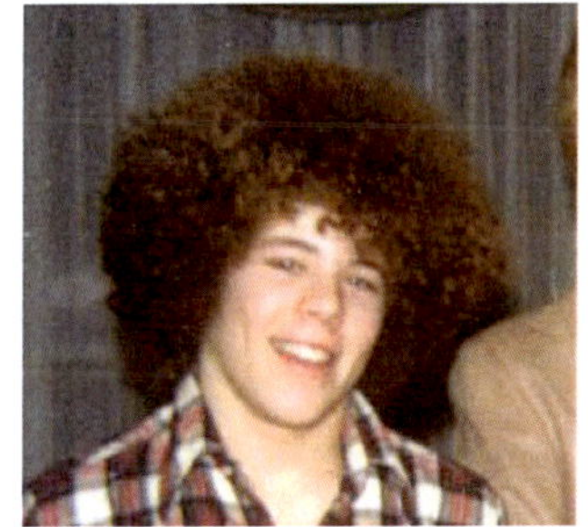

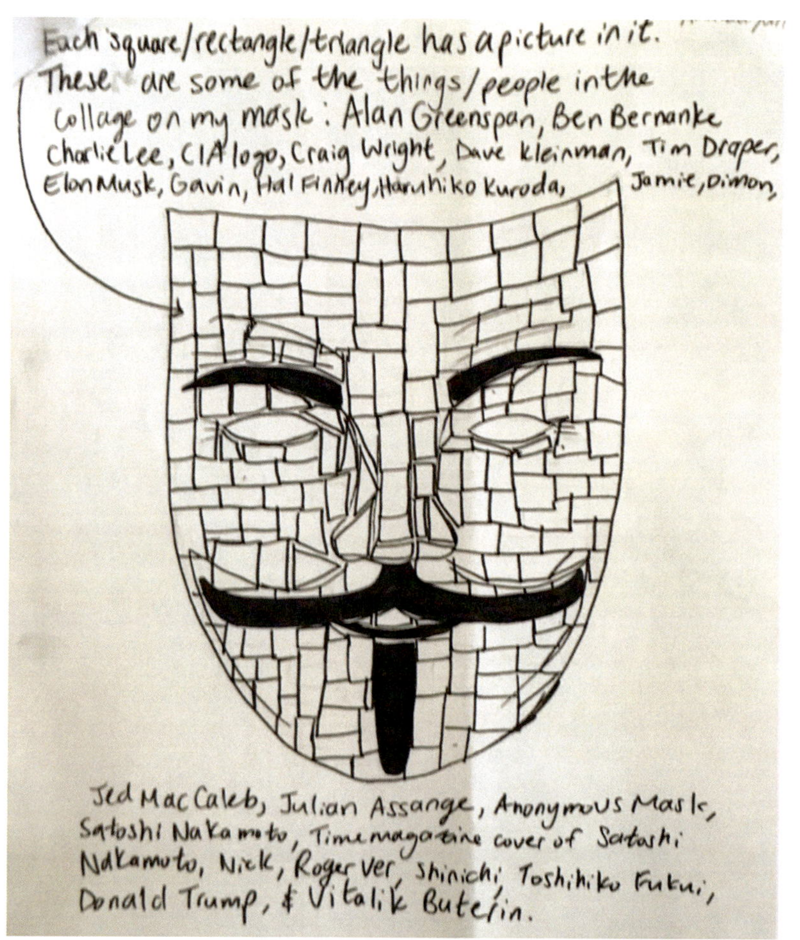

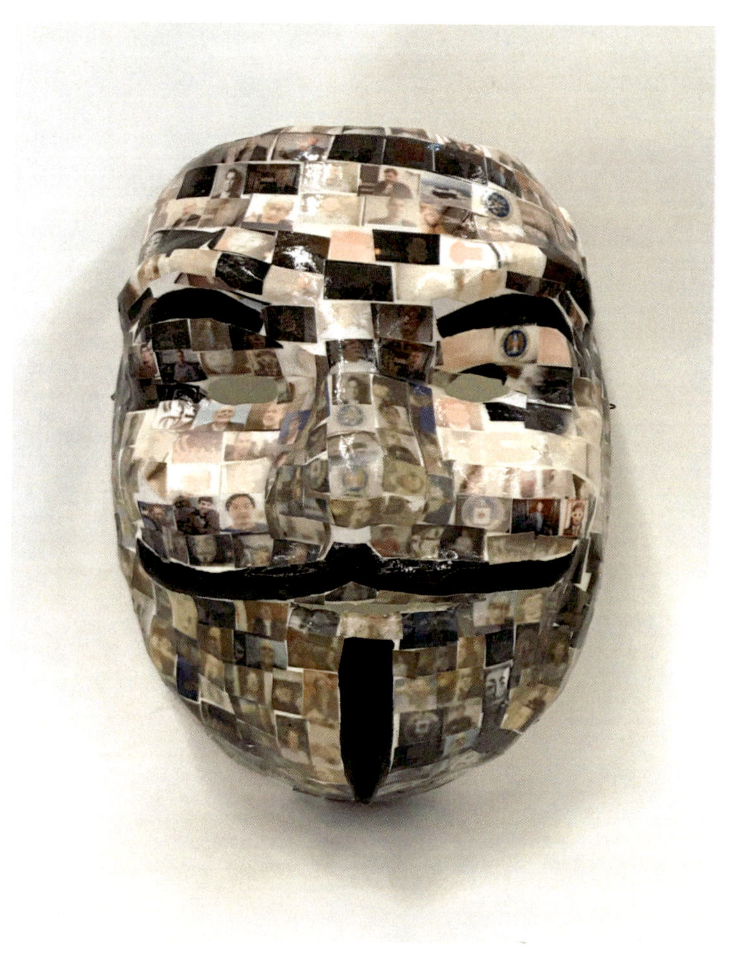

I don't even remember this kid, but if this is what they were into in 8th grade, I am quite sure they've gone on to do amazing things.

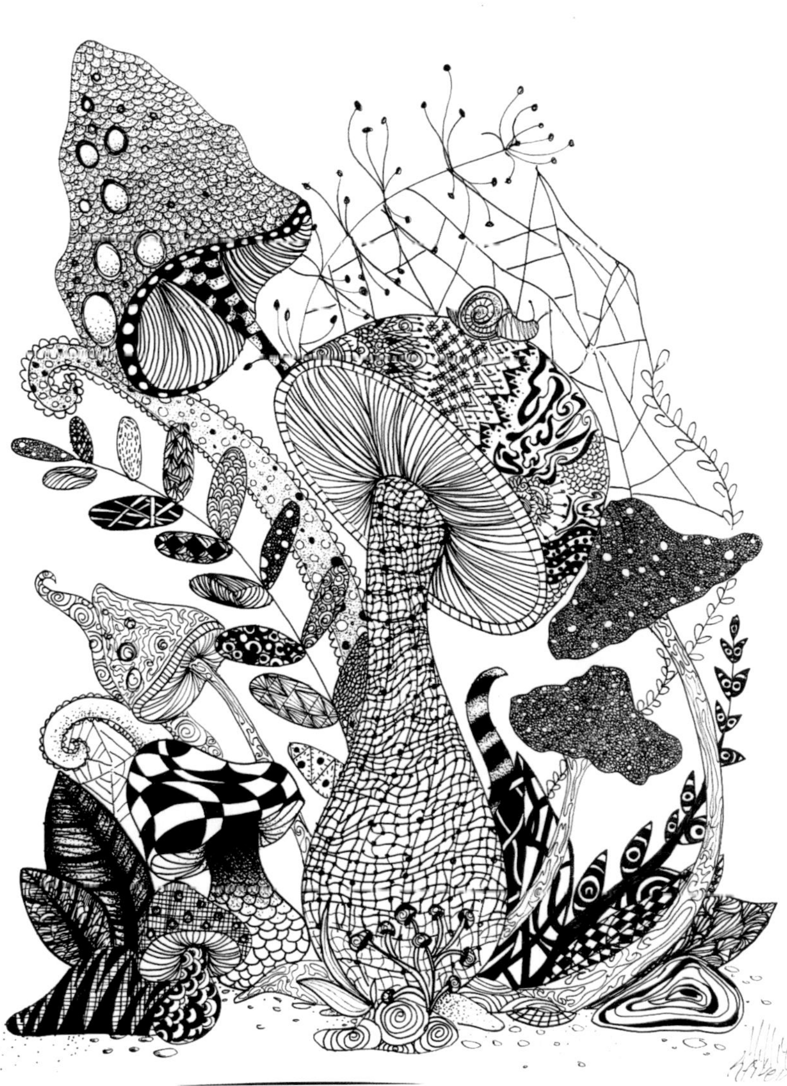

Kid #1: What do you want to be when you grow up?

Kid #2: I want to be Mario.

Kid #1: Your aspiration in life is to be a middle-aged Italian plumber?

Kid shows up in class with a tray of absolutely gorgeous cupcakes:

Kid: Mr. G., would you like a cupcake?

Me: Of course. These look great! Did you make these yourself?

Kid: Yeah, I was really nervous because my bar mitzvah is next weekend and when I get really nervous, I bake.

Kid: I'm not sure what I should say on my Mother's Day card.

Me: How about "Dear Mom: I want you to know how much I love you, value you, and appreciate everything you have done for me."

Kid: That's debatable.

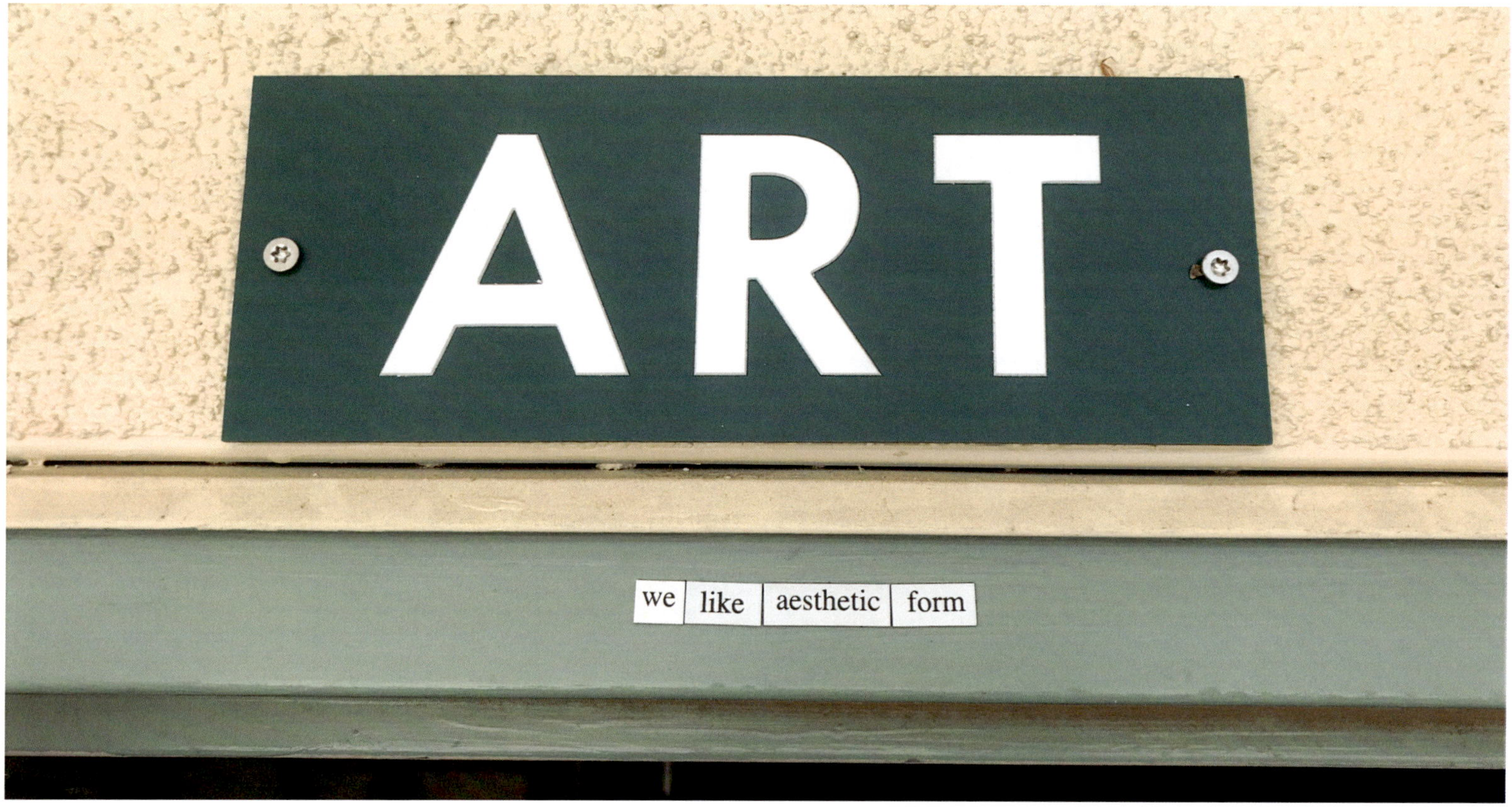

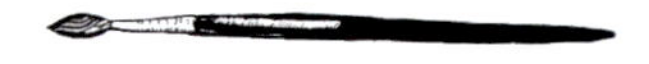

Kid: Life at home is so weird right now. My mom just figured out how to use emojis.

Me: Which US agency comes after you if you counterfeit currency?

Kid: Barbra Streisand.

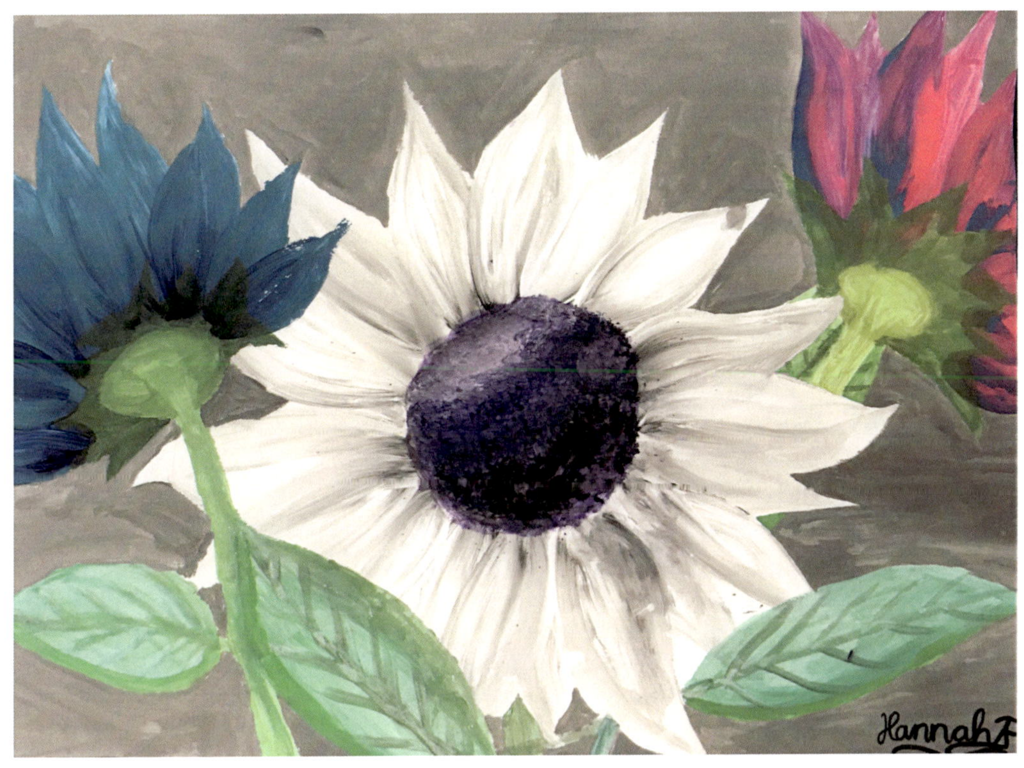

Me: How does your finished ceramic box reflect who you are?

Kid: Like me, this box is a hot mess.

Kid is riding through the parking lot with no helmet:
Me: Where's your helmet?
Kid: *sigh, eye roll* I'm just going to the back of the school.
Me: I care about your head.
Kid: The only time I've ever fallen off my bike was when I had training wheels.

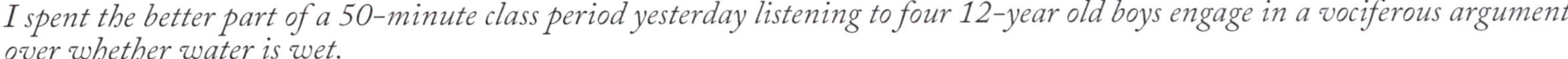

Me: You should not be watching Ariana Grande's new video – it's full of inappropriate language.

Kid: Mr. G., you're forgetting about pretty much the rest of the internet.

I spent the better part of a 50-minute class period yesterday listening to four 12-year old boys engage in a vociferous argument over whether water is wet.

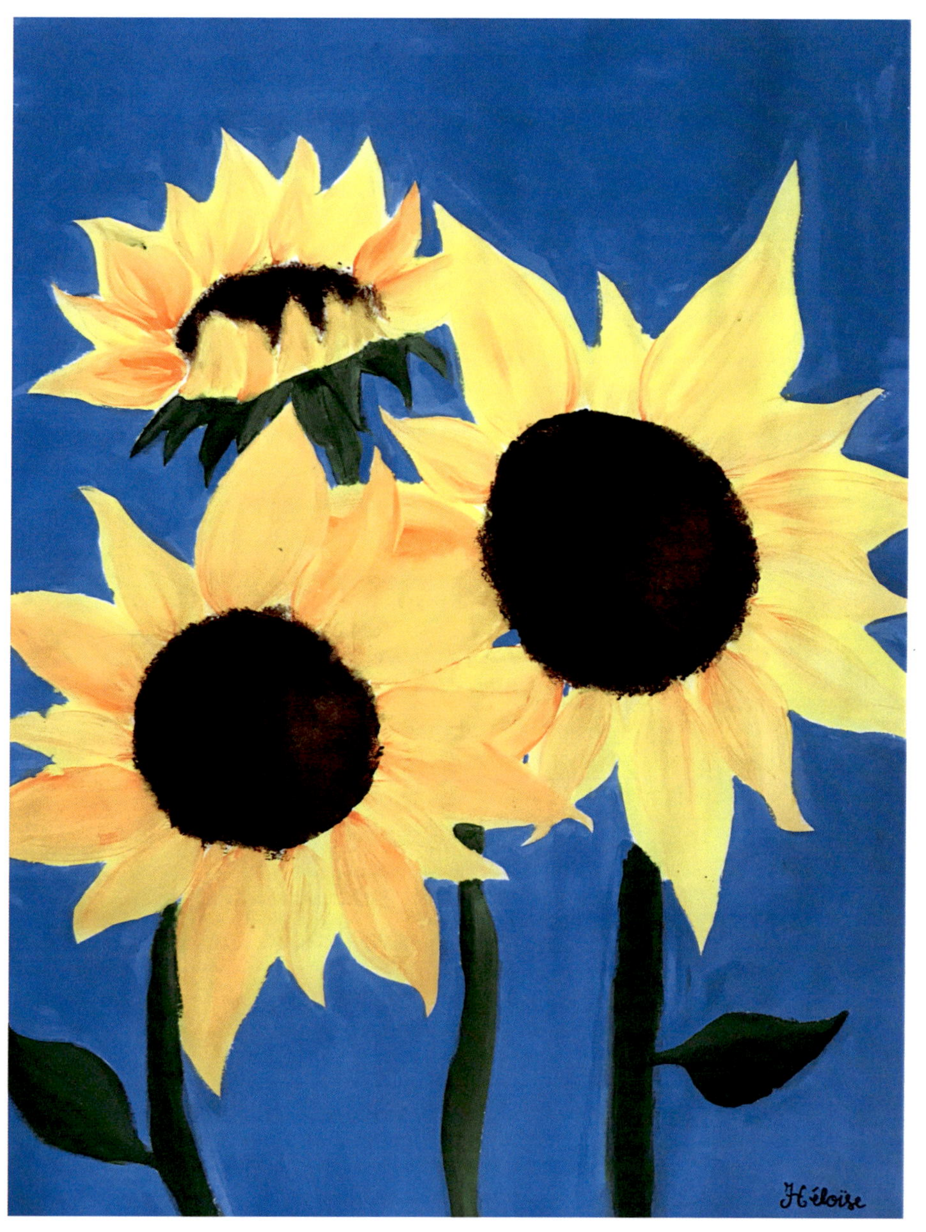

 Can't Keep My Hands to Myself *is playing on Spotify and I hear one of my kids muttering to himself in response to the lyrics:*

Kid: This is not healthy behavior, please see a therapist.

Me: Stop standing around like a bunch of sheep.

Kid: I am a sheep.

Me: No, you're not. Sheep are really stupid. You're not stupid.

Kid: Yes I am. Last week I asked my dad what Justin Bieber's last name was.

Kid: Mr. G., do you have any old school music?

Me: Depends on your definition of "old school."

Kid: Like Tupac.

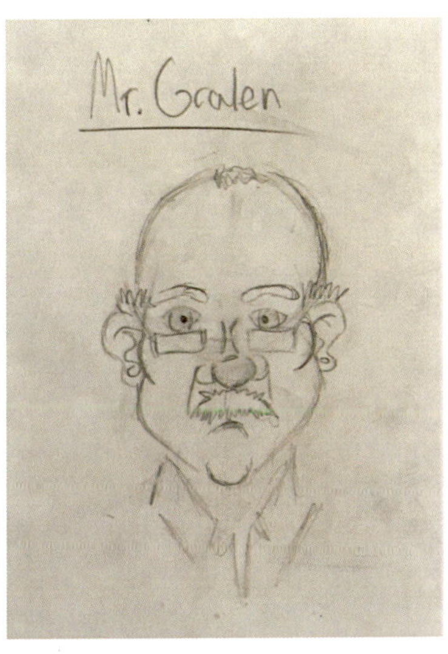

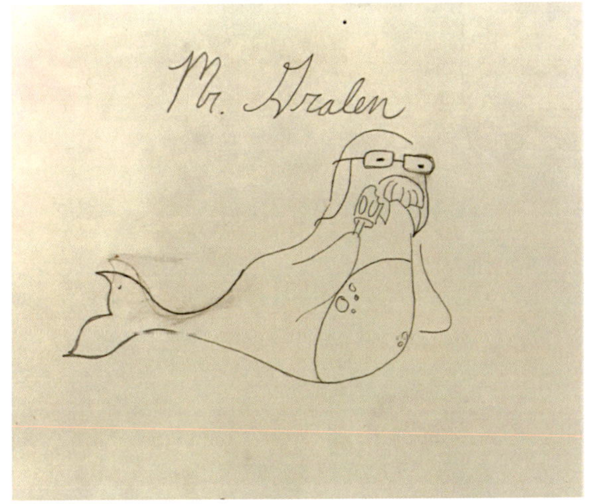

Kid: Where can I find a pencil?

Me: Right in front of you. It's amazing how you can find a pencil in an art classroom. Along with paint and paint brushes. Stuff like that. Usually right in front of you.

Kid: I'm hearing some serious sass coming from you, Mr. G.

Reason #482 why I love my job: I have two kids who are fiercely determined to try to cook a chicken in the kiln.

Overheard:

Kid: Tylenol fixes everything. Headache? Try Tylenol. Joints aching? Give Tylenol a try. Broken marriage? Why not see if Tylenol works?

Perennially late kid was tardy again today. I asked her if she had trouble getting out of bed:

Kid: No, this time it was my dad's fault. He threw a tantrum in the car.

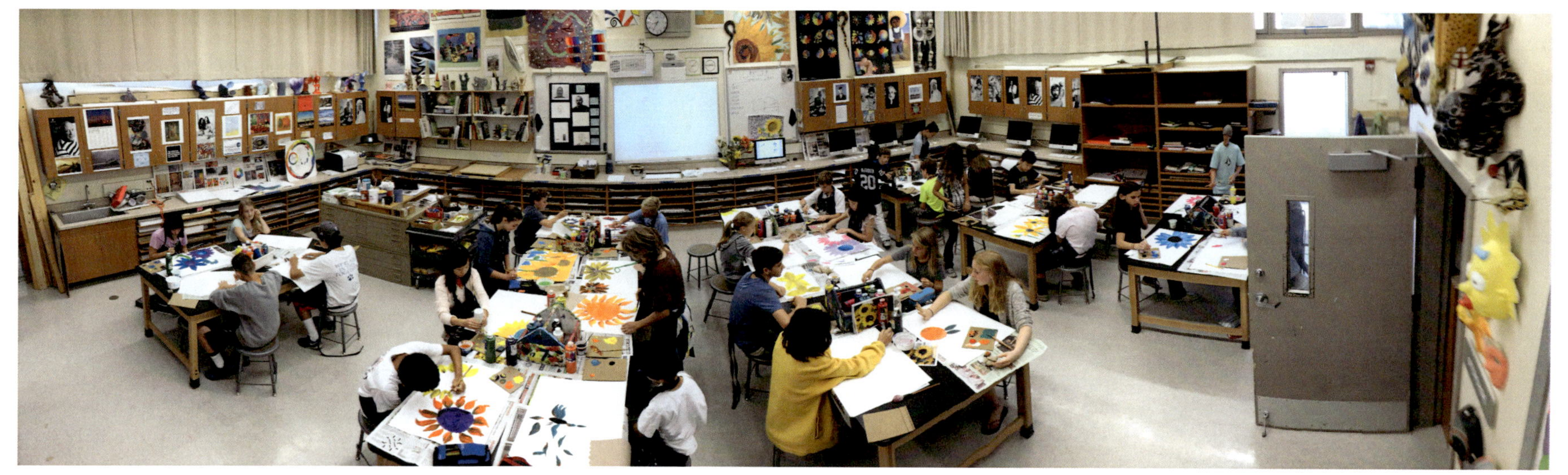

Sunflowers!

I had occasion to use the phrase "Don't look a gift horse in the mouth" in class this morning:

Me: Does anyone know where that saying comes from?

Kid: Nebraska?

Kid is carving a ceramic piece but the clay is too dry:

Me: Don't carve it when it's that dry. You're creating dust that's unhealthy.

Kid: We're all going to die eventually anyway.

Me: Well, that escalated quickly.

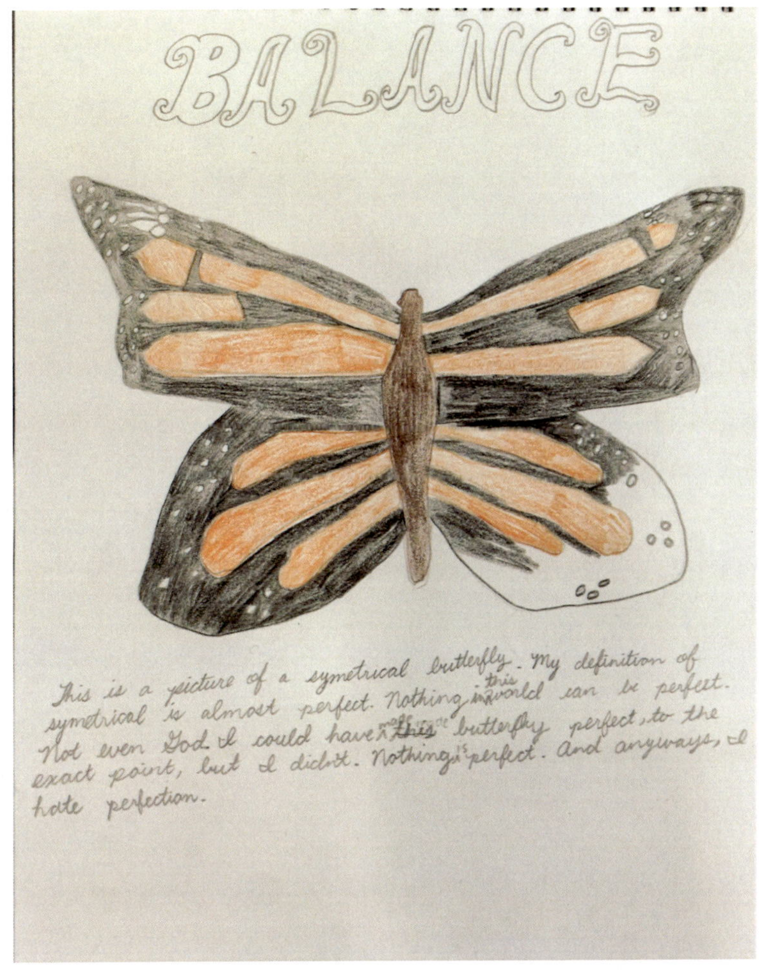

"This is a picture of a symetrical butterfly. My definition of symetrical is almost perfect. Nothing in this world can be perfect. Not even God. I could have made the butterfly perfect, to the exact point, but I didn't. Nothing is perfect. And anyways, I hate perfection."

I was telling the kids that I like to listen to podcasts and music when I go out for a walk:

Kid: Why would anyone walk voluntarily?

Kid: My mom took my phone away and we argued every day for a week.

Me: You're in the "You-Are-Not-The-Boss-Of-Me" phase, right?

Kid: That's the story of my life.

Kid #1: My mom took away my PS4 and I don't even know what to do.

Kid #2: It's called going outside.

I made three kids move about 150 pounds of clay for me this morning. (I know, I'm a slave driver):

Me: Was that good exercise for you?

Kid: THAT STAINED MY LULU LEMON PANTS. *Pause* Wow, that must be the most white girl thing I've ever said!

Remember that you need to do a full color, full-page drawing of your mask as well.

Write your paragraph here:

My mask has a lot of texture that I created with plaster to form wings. On the wings I added small lines of gold to add more detail. I made angel wings because not only do they represent peace and happiness but angels are also known for bringing messages of truth to aid mankind. My mask is a reminder to help those in need and also to know that somewhere in the distance guardians are looking out for us all for better and safer lives.

Kid is working in our room at lunch on a project for another class:
Kid: Now comes the fun part of my project: extinction! I get to draw burning dinosaurs, dying animals, and an erupting volcano!

Kid: I can't do this.

Me: You're not allowed to say "can't" in here.

Kid: How about "won't"?

Me: Are you in a "you-are-not-the-boss-of-me" fight with your parents these days?

Kid: Yeah, but that's a snap. If you pick the right argument, you can just use their own words against them.

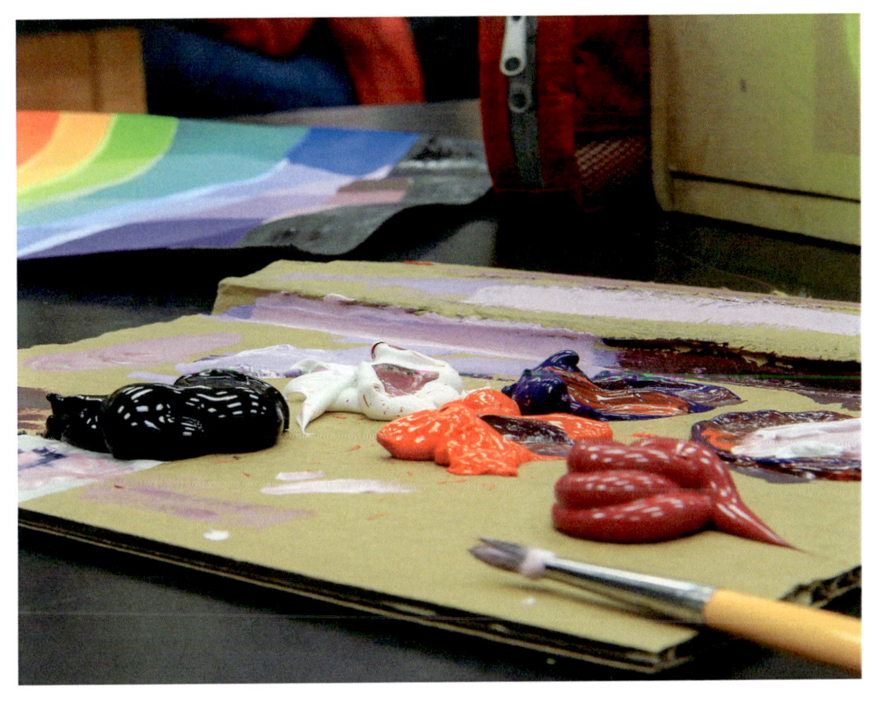

Kid: If I ever get a pet pig, I'm going to name him Chris P. Bacon.

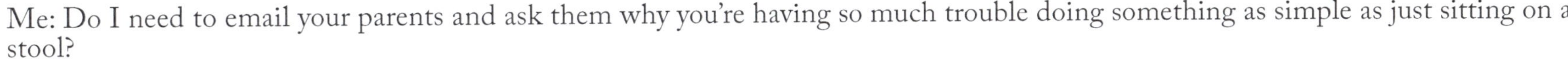

Me: I have great faith in your generation. You are going to change the world.

Kid: What are we gonna do?

Me: You're going to invent faster-than-light travel so we can visit other star systems.

Kid: And then we can get away from Donald Trump.

Kid #1: I think I need to retire.

Me: You've got a ways to go yet, kiddo, just hang in there.

Kid #2: Wait, Mr. G., what happens to you when you're an art teacher and you get too old to function?

Me: Well, that escalated quickly.

Me: Do I need to email your parents and ask them why you're having so much trouble doing something as simple as just sitting on a stool?

Kid: They wouldn't be surprised at all.

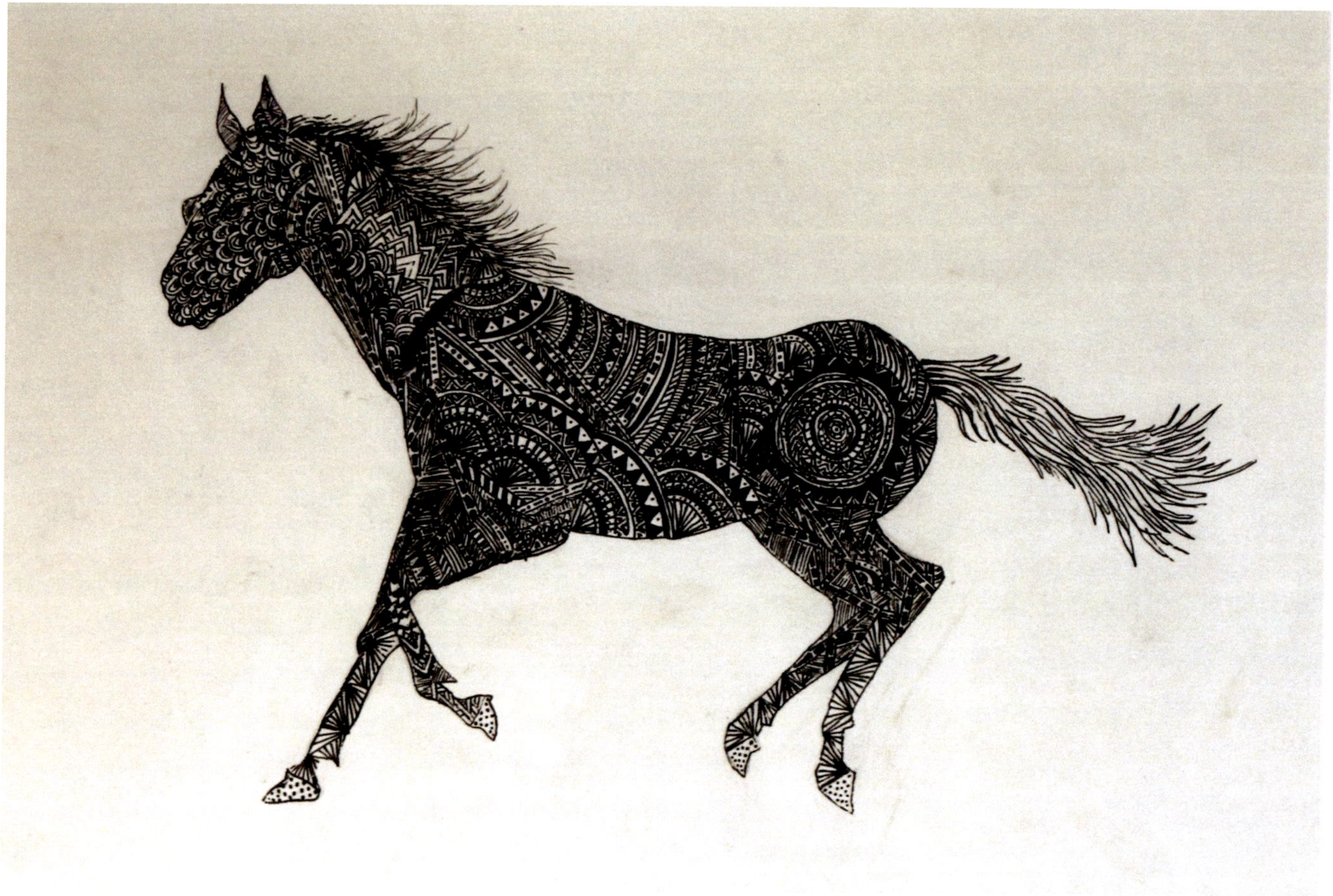

Me: Sharing is caring.

Kid: If there's a zombie apocalypse, it won't really matter.

Me: How many of your parents regulate your hours on your phone?

Kid: My parents are scared of phones.

Kid: I like math a lot more than social studies because in math there's only one right answer.

Q: What was the most interesting part of this project? (You must use the term "LOL" at least once in your response.)

A: It's how I combined and jumbled two design concepts to represent the chaos and corruption in society and government and how we are all doomed to a violent death. LOL.

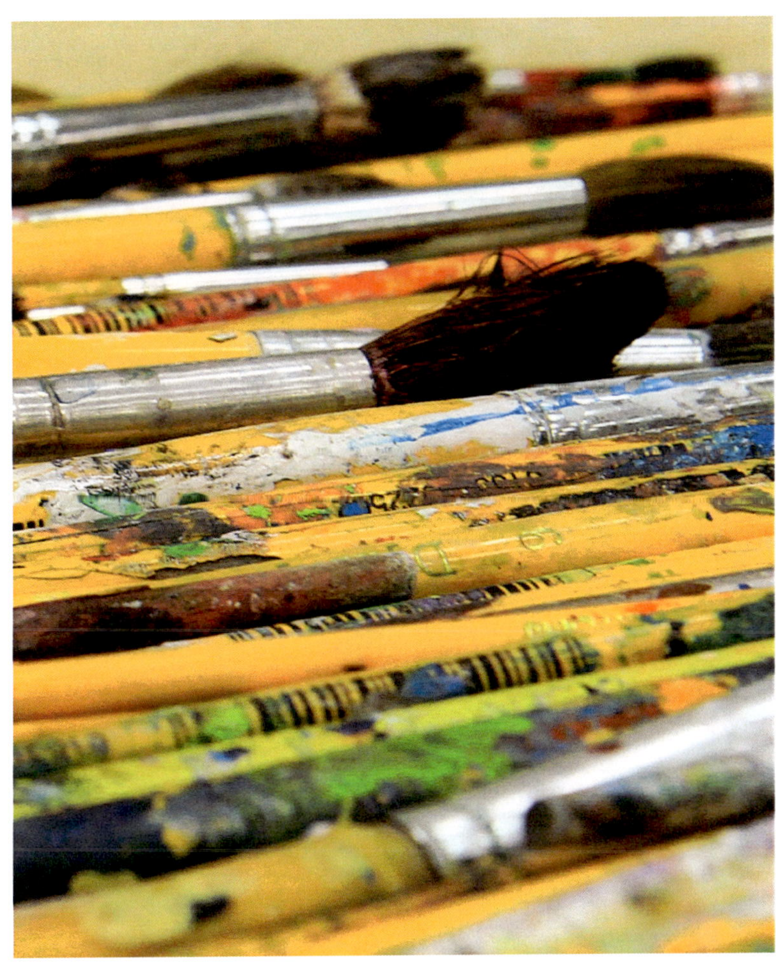

Kid is laying out an incredibly detailed and complicated color wheel and asks my advice:

Me: Well, you've created quite a challenge for yourself here.

Kid: "Challenge" is my middle name.

Kid #1: Mr. G, why aren't you doing "Dress Alike" like everyone else?

Me: I have a pathological antipathy toward dressing like everyone else because I had to wear a uniform as a Catholic schoolboy.

Kid #2: I don't understand a single word you just said.

Kid #3: That means you really don't like it, right?

Me: I'm going to be coming around taking pictures of hands doing this drawing, so don't be shy. No one can tell who you are from a picture of your hands.

Kid: What about Donald Trump?

Me: Do something helpful at home without being asked and see what happens.

Kid: My parents would completely lose their minds.

39

Kid: I would love to be there when you play Fergalicious for your father.

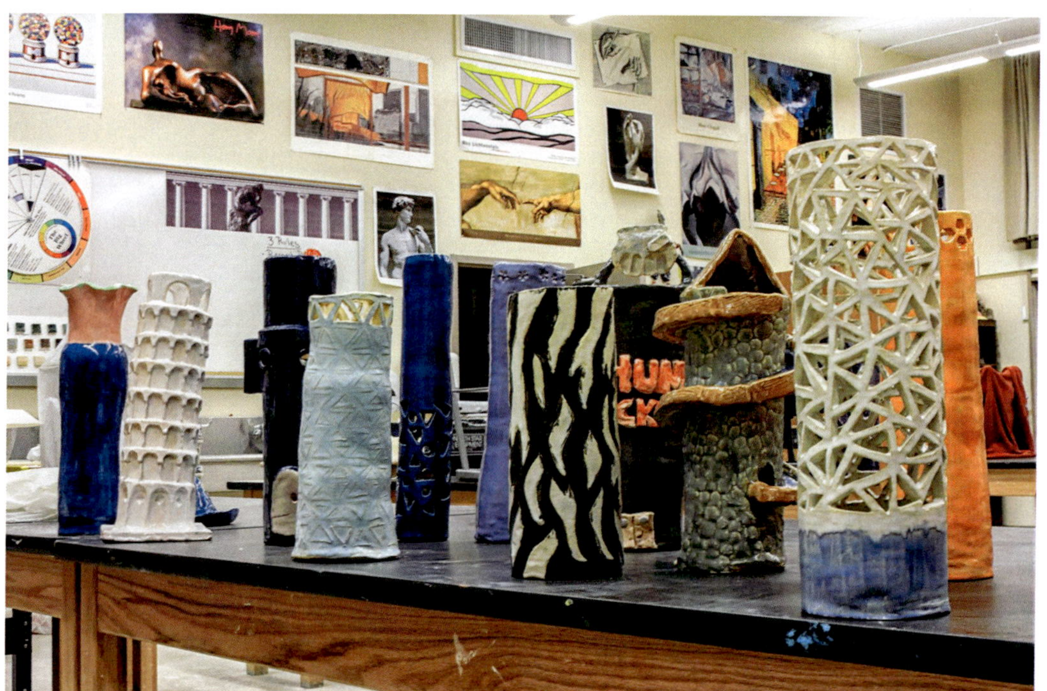

Me: Eventually dabbing will be like Vine and it will die.

Kid: That was too soon, Mr. Gralen.

I was showing my students a cool animated video that depicted cholesterol in the bloodstream:

Me: That's cholesterol. That's the bad stuff."

Kid: There's good cholesterol and bad cholesterol, Mr. G. You can't generalize like that or you're being cholesterolist.

I do a very short mindfulness practice at the beginning of every class. Today my 8th graders in Ceramics were very squirrelly, a couple of boys especially:

Me: Jeez, you guys. The 6th graders are better at this than you are.

Kid: They don't have as much testosterone as we do.

Me: Remember, your drawing has to have at least three adjectives on it describing your awesome self.

Kid: Can I use "Kanye"?

Me: Kanye is not an adjective. Kanye is an idiot.

Kid: OK, how about "Pablo"?

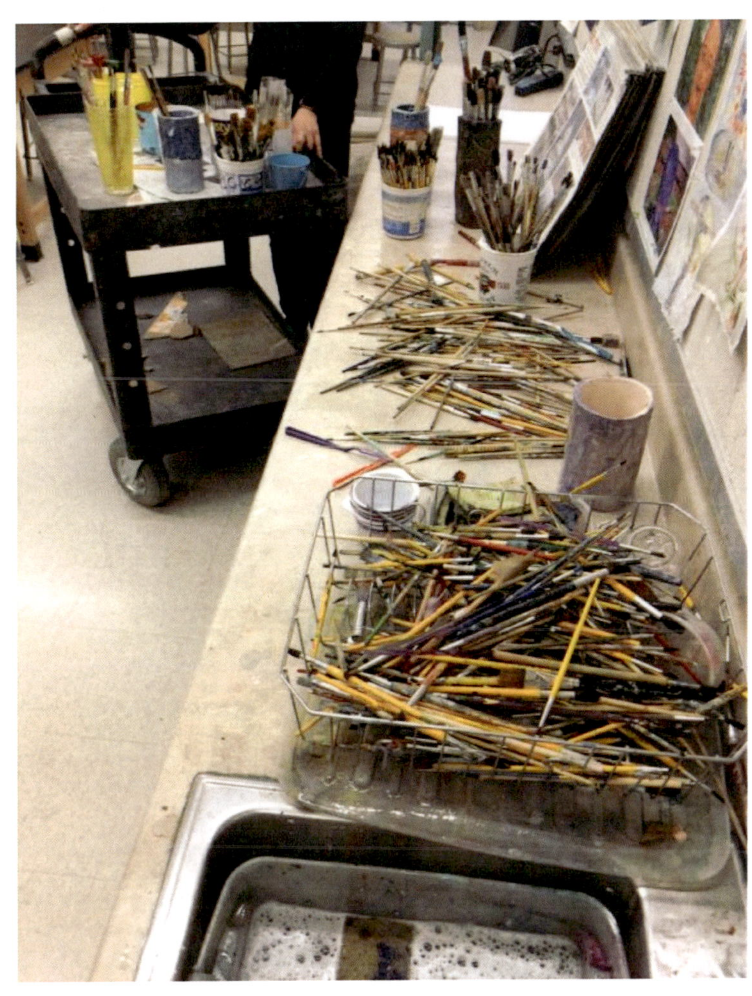

So. Many. Paintbrushes.

Kid #1: Would you rather turn into a pumpkin or an eggplant?

Kid #2: It depends. Would I be, like, conscious?

Kid: Would you rather be gored to death by a unicorn or fall out of a 50th floor window?

Kid #1: Do you have a talent?

Kid #2: I do. It's called hiding and never coming out.

Kid #3: Just like my dad.

You overhear the weirdest stuff in the middle school classroom. A bunch of kids are working on some sort of collage:

Kid #1 to Kid #2: That looks like the she-male version of Abraham Lincoln.

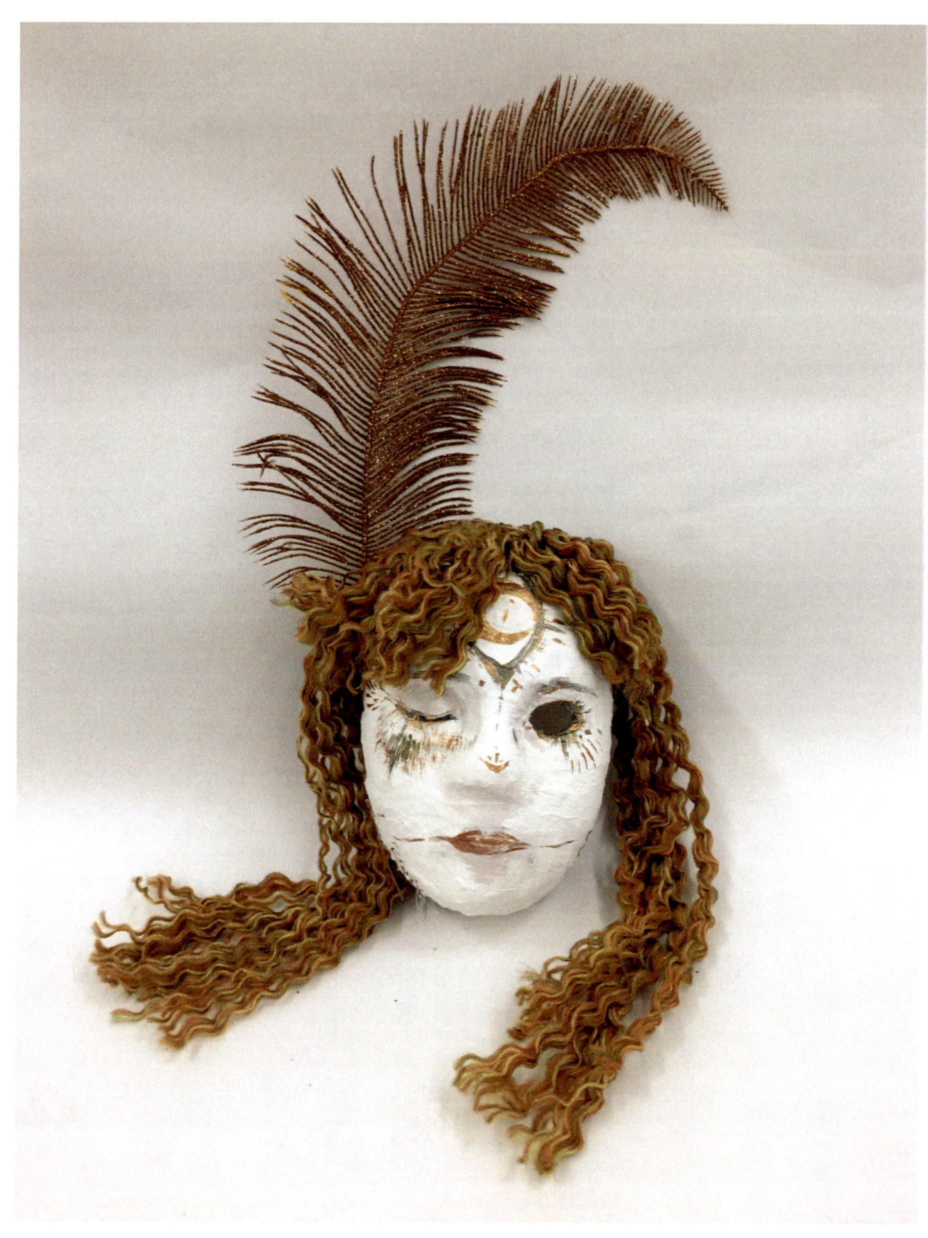

Me: Have any of you guys seen "Batman vs. Superman"?

Kid: I did. For the first two hours it was kinda boring.

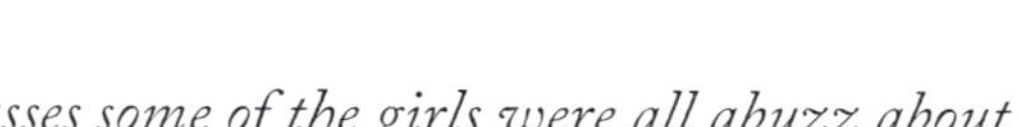

In two of my classes some of the girls were all abuzz about a particular boy who's had a very scratchy, croaky voice all semester. Evidently it changed overnight to a bass:

Kid: Yeah, he went through puberty.

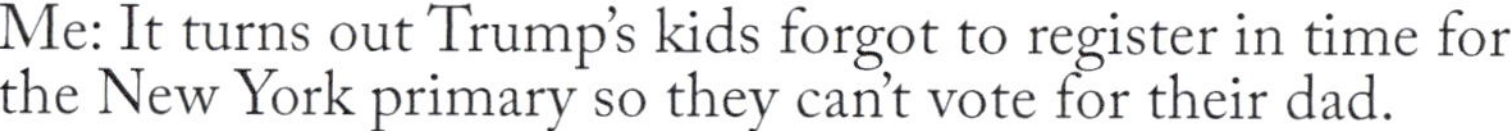

Me: It turns out Trump's kids forgot to register in time for the New York primary so they can't vote for their dad.

Kid: Maybe they don't really WANT to vote for him, and this is their way of getting out of it.

I'm playing my Lady Gaga stream on Pandora in the classroom, and a Rihanna tune comes on. This kid gets all excited:

Kid: You got some good music going on here, Mr. G. This is from my childhood.

Me: Which is happening right now, right?

Kid: I'M THIRTEEN.

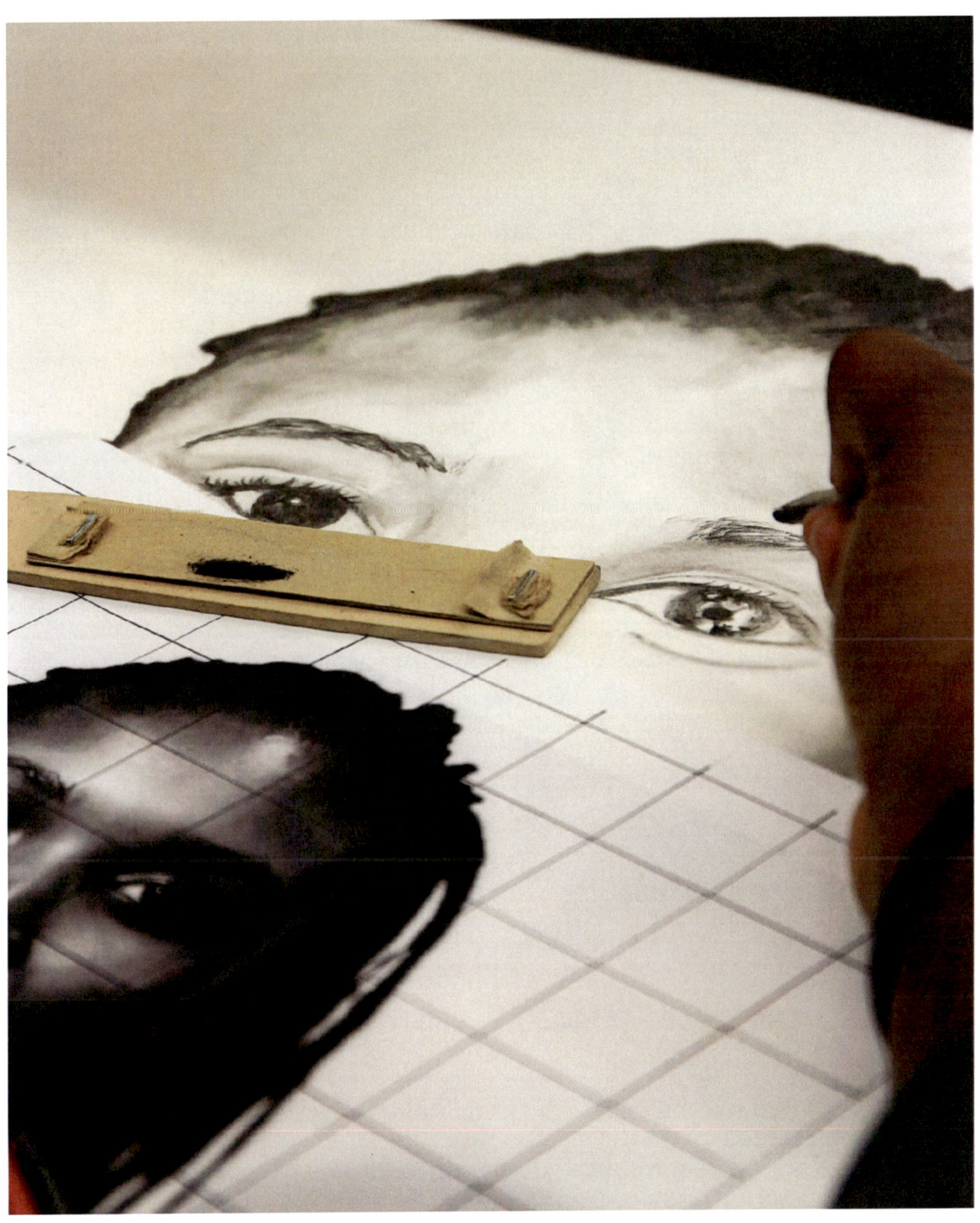

Kid #1: Do we have to go to graduation?

Kid #2: What do you have going on that's more important than graduating?

Kid #1: Tennis.

Q: What was the most interesting part of this project and why was it interesting to you?

A: The most interesting part of this project is that I went against the instructions and made my own project, which allowed me to think for myself.

OK, I can't really argue with that.

We are doing digital self-portraits in art class:

Kid: I am not sure if eyelashes are hair.

Me: Yes, they are.

Kid: No, they're not. They're a gift from the Illuminati.

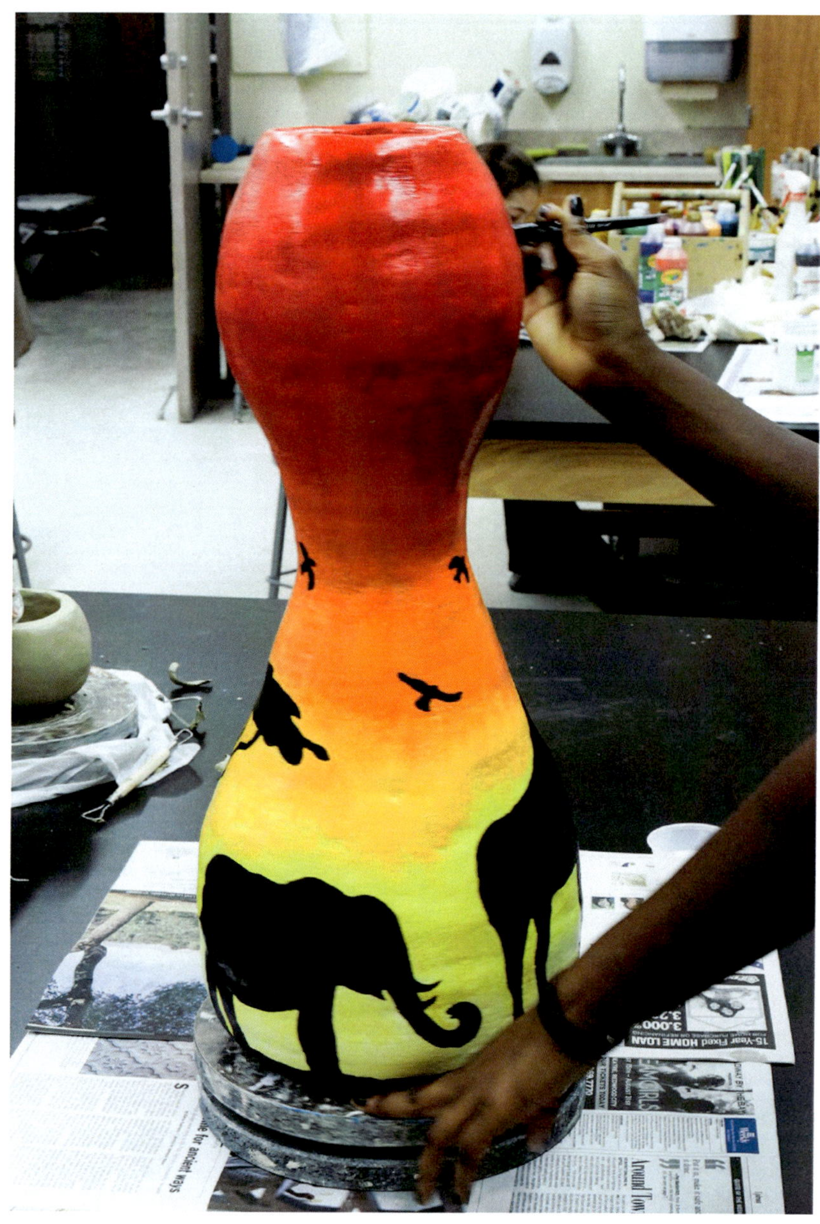

Kid: Mr. G., my parents made me go to the opera yesterday.

Me: What did you see?

Kid: Carmen.

Me: Did you enjoy it?

Kid: The music was OK I guess, but the story was just cheesy.

There is a move afoot to re-name our school. I am soliciting input from the kids: after all, it's their school.

Best suggestion so far: *Jerry Garcia Middle School*

The day after the Super Bowl 50:

Me: If you steal my pencils, I will be sadder than Cam Newton.

Kid: WHY WOULD YOU SAY THAT?

Me: None of you are wearing aprons! Your mom is going to be really mad at me when you get paint all over your clothes.

Kid: We could sign waivers for that.

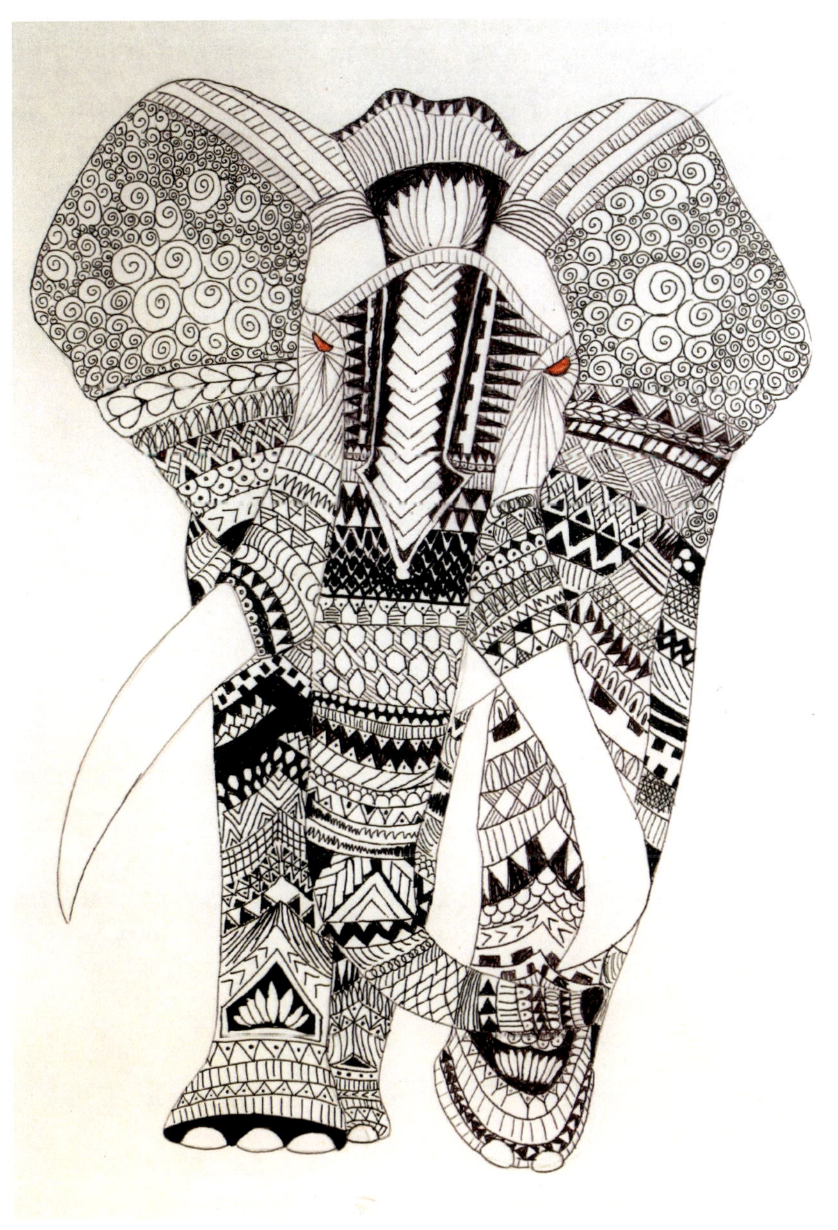

Me: Just think – you'll be able to look back at this picture in twenty years and remember how cute you were at this age!

Kid: And then we'll cry, because we'll be old.

When I think of Paris, I think of there beautiful arts like cooking (Cooking is an ART). And when I think of cooking I think of food. Pizza. Pasta. Baguettes. Gnocchi. Macaroons. Have you ever heard the phrase: When in Paris eat good food. Well if you haven't then learn it now cause Paris has some typical foods which you must try or else you will die. La Fin. (P.S. that means the end in French.)

Kid: I don't think that's a very good idea. I like his income the way it is now.

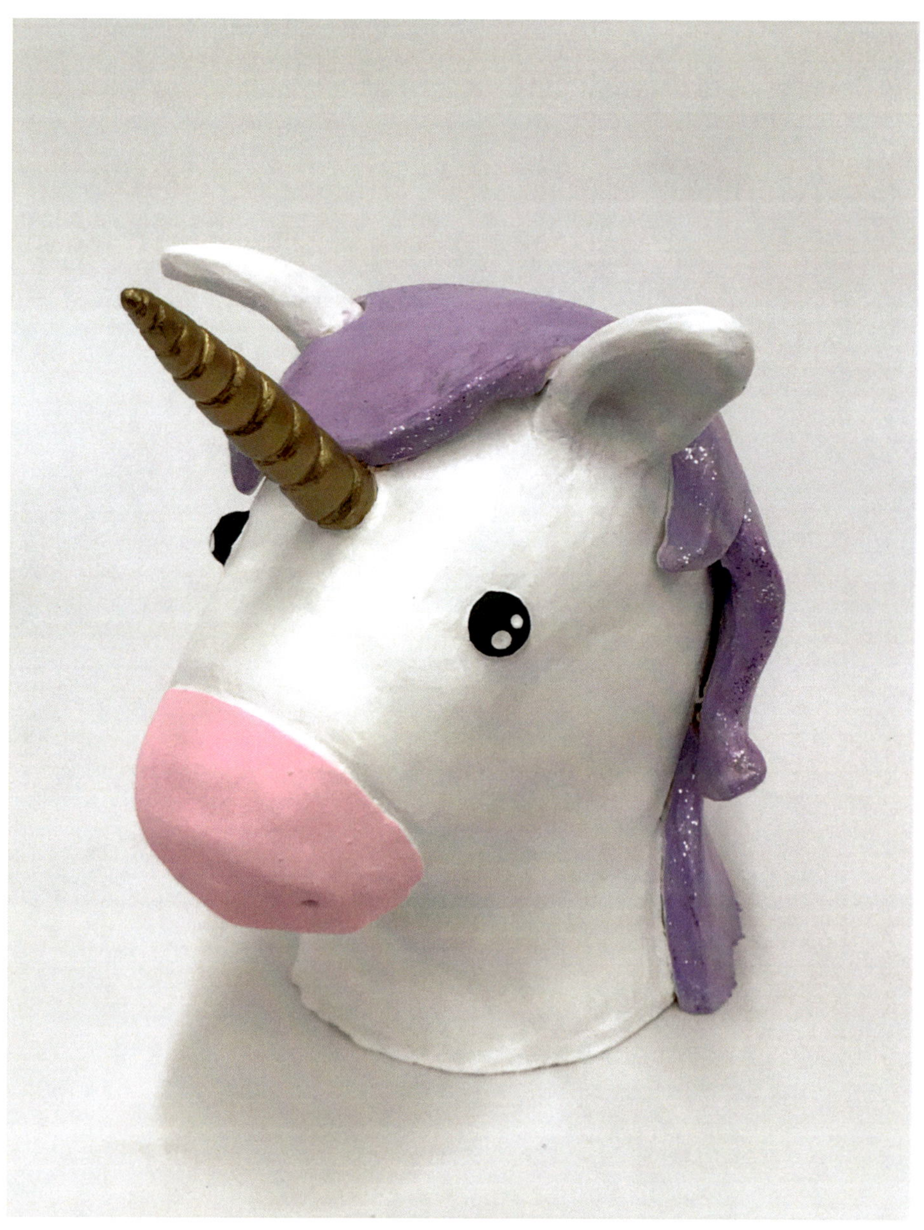

Me: Spoiler alert – you're probably going to come across some highly inappropriate images if you are looking at Bosch.

Kid: Tell me about it. I've already seen about two hundred nudists.

Me to a stubborn kid: You just have to broaden your horizons. You're like a flat earther on a spherical world. If you keep going, you're eventually going to come back around to where you started from.

Kid: You just made something really simple into something really deep.

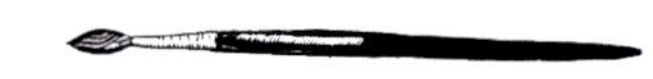

Me: This is called a "truncated icosahedron, a type of Archimedean solid."

Kid: I've heard of that.

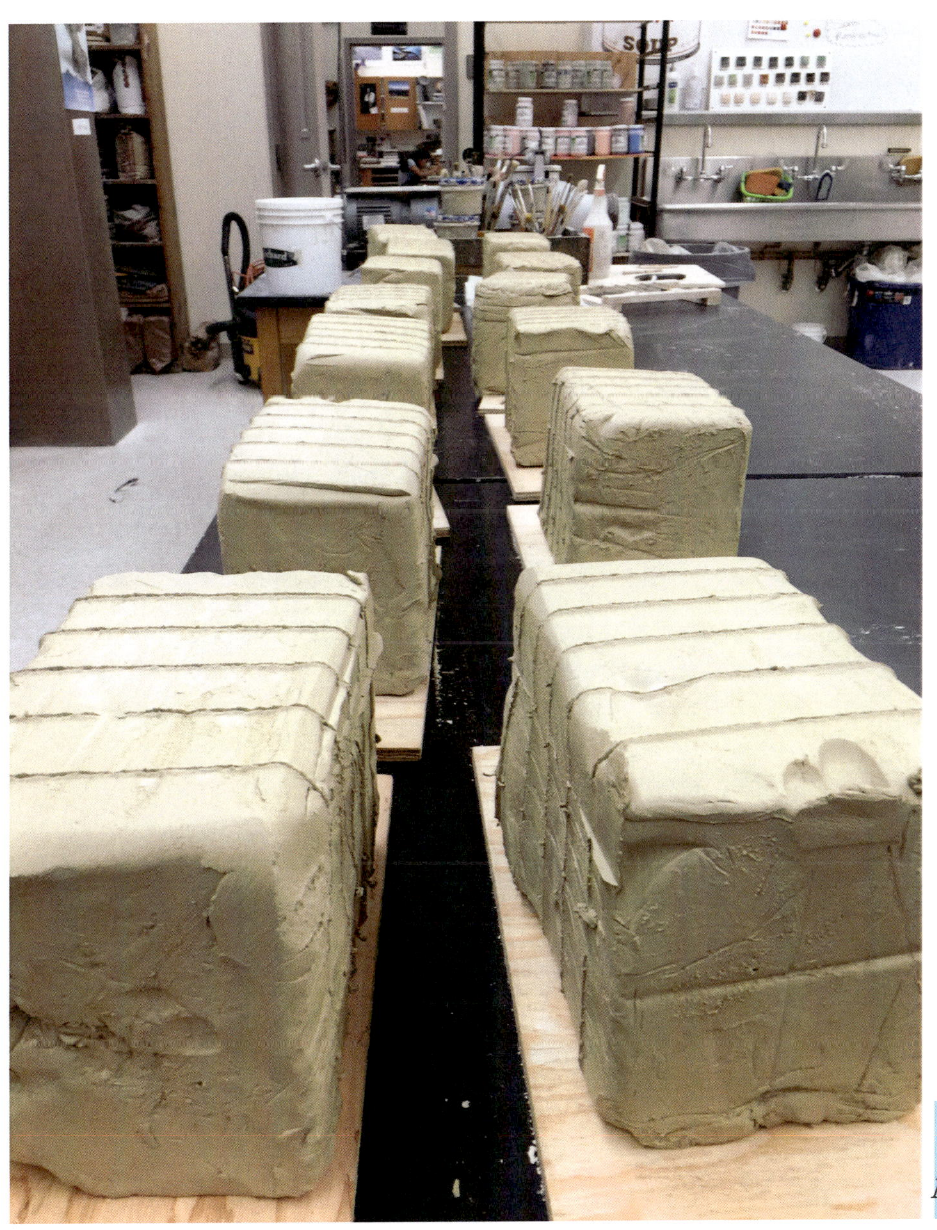

Me: Do I look like I was born yesterday?

Kid: No. You're bald but you have a mustache.

Overheard:

Kid: OK, question for all you guys: Can you see "Barney's Great Adventure" being made into a horror film?

Girl is being kinda mean to the boy:

Me: You need to be nice to him. He's a gentleman. That's rare.

Girl: I just like messing with him. And chasing him with a hammer.

Boy: You sound like my sister.

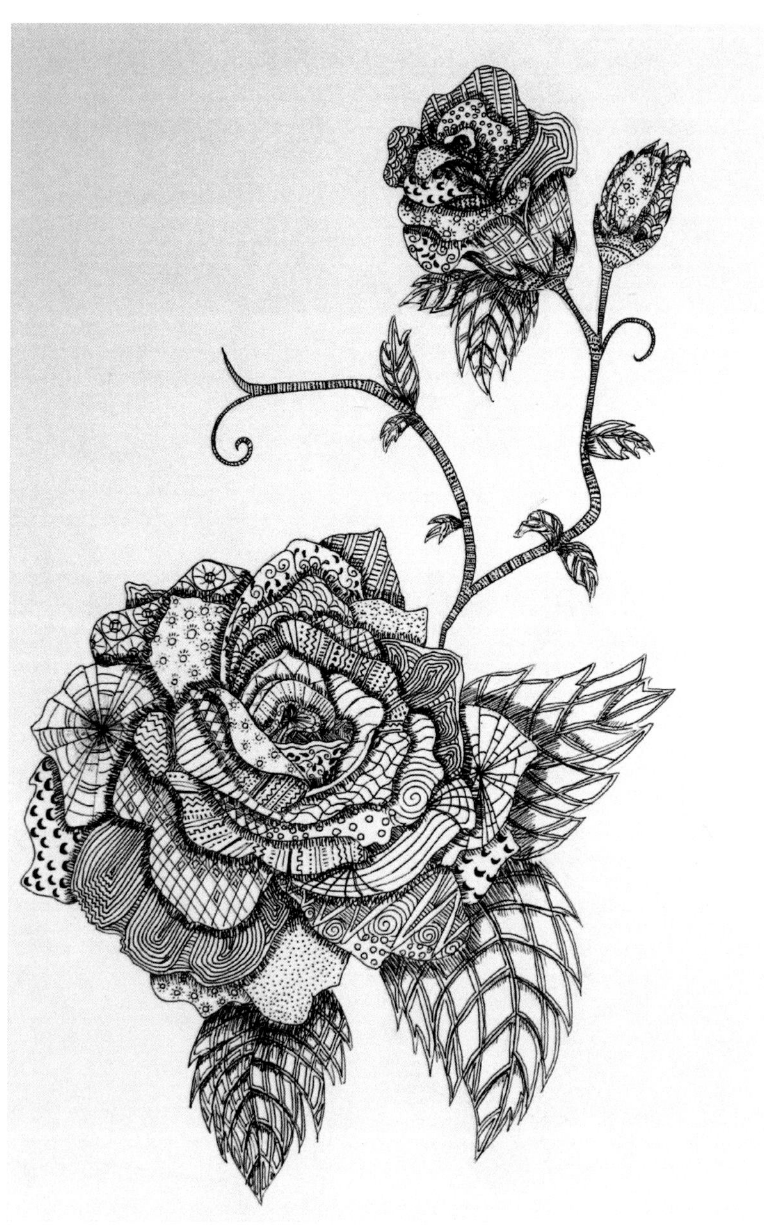

Kid: Is Ceramics class fun, Mr. G.?

Me: No, it's a miserable, ruinous experience. That's why so many kids signed up for it.

Kid: You're really good at sarcasm.

Kid: Mr. G., do you have any children?

Me: No, I have 150 children here and then I go home alone at night.

Kid: And take some Advil?

The subtleties of art vocabulary:

Kid: Mr. Gralen, where is the tempura paint?

Me: Are you looking for Japanese food or art supplies?

Overheard in the the 6th grade classroom:

Kid: Why is Christmas just like a day at the office? You do all the work and the fat guy with the suit gets all the credit.

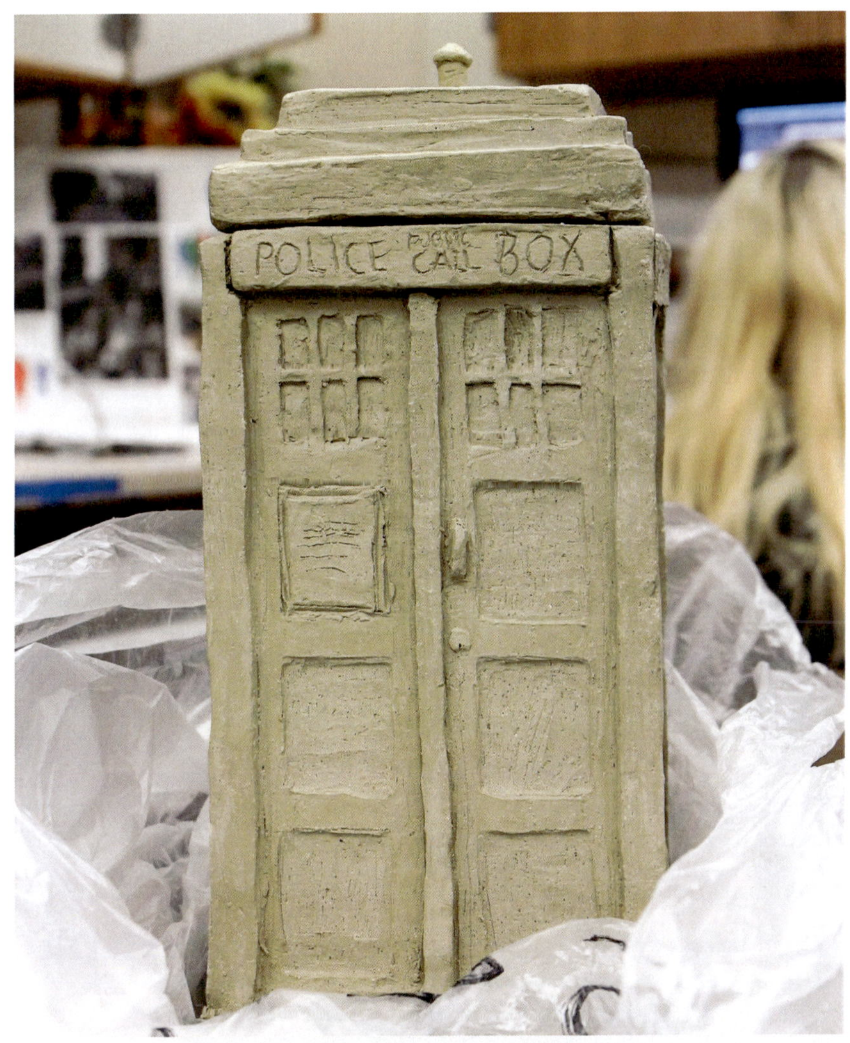

Your ceramic box can be any kind of design you want.

OH OH OH OH OH! I'M MAKING A TARDIS!

There's always that one kid who is way ahead of the game:

Q: What did you like best about this project?

A: Even if you do absolutely terrible work, you can pass it off as "modern art" – that way no one can criticize you.

I'm moving a huge pot that this kid is making:

Me: Geez, you guys are killing me with all these big coil pots.

Kid: But we believe in you, Mr. G.!

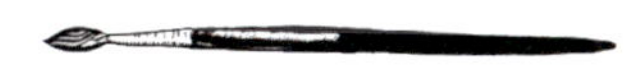

Me: Your next project is an acrylic self-portrait on canvas. When you are done you will have a permanent record of how lovely you were at this age.

Kid: But Mr. G., we've already got Instagram!

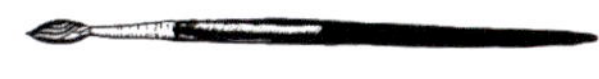

Kid: Mr. G., where do you keep your pencil supply? You'll notice I'm not asking if I can have a pencil.

Me: You will make a great lawyer.

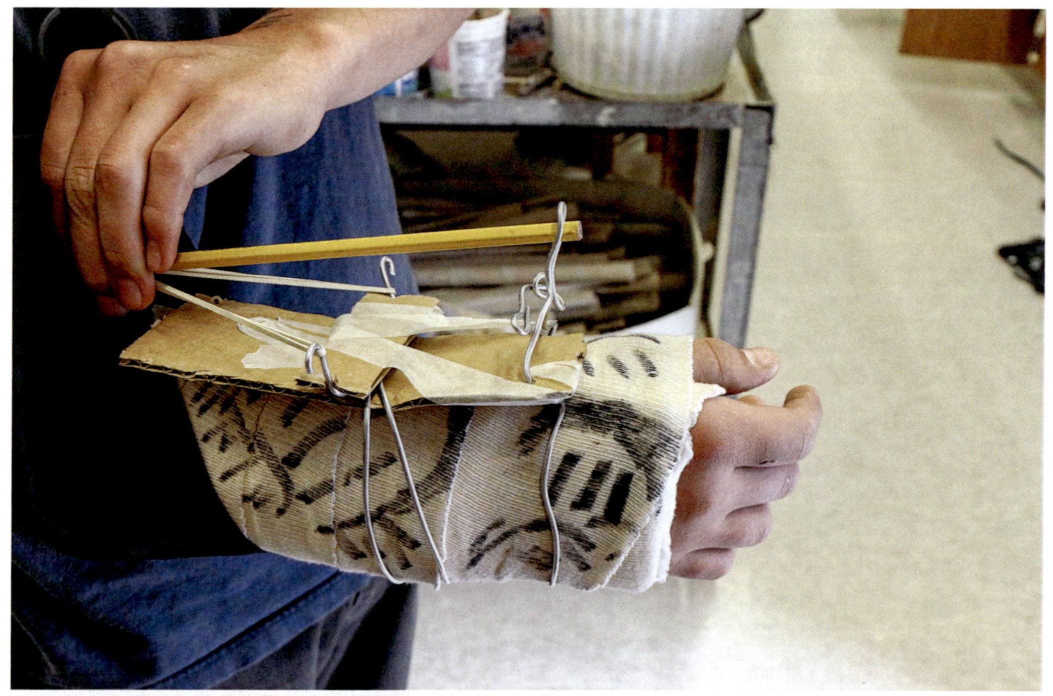

The kid who broke his arm gets a pass on most of our class activities, for obvious reasons. But he's been teaching himself how to draw ambidextrously, and then he made a catapult. With one hand.

Kid is making a huge mess at her table:

Me: Why do you not have some newspaper on the table, like we always do?

Kid: I like living on the edge, Mr. G.

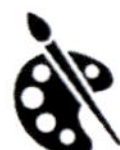

Overheard during clean-up:

Kid: We should have scented tables.

Me: You guys are so weird.

Kid: But that's a good thing, right?

Kid: Mr. G., I need some advice on how to get my phone back – my mom took it away.

Me: Why did she take it?

Kid: Well, we were having a conversation, but I wasn't yelling TOO much, and then she got mad and took it.

Me: Yelling is not a "conversation," and is probably not a good strategy anyway. Maybe you should try being nice to her.

Kid: Your advice is always so hard.

Kid: Mr. G., I don't think I can do this.

Me: Did you even try?

Kid: No.

Me: You have to try.

Kid: This trying thing is really difficult.

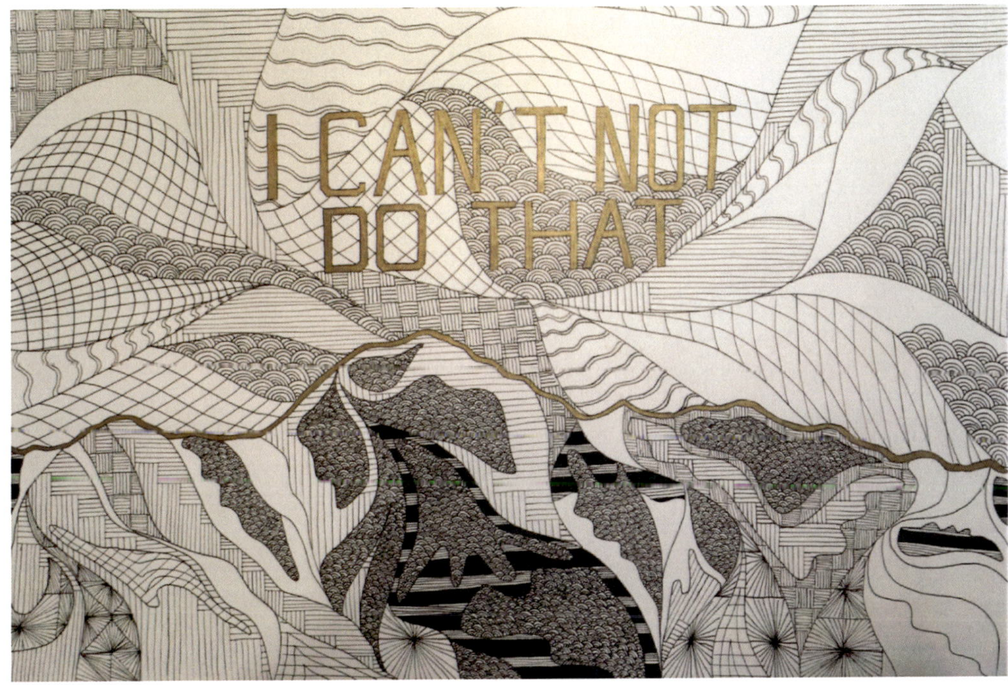

Overheard in the classroom this morning, one kid to another:
"Seriously? Did your mother drop you on your head when you were a baby?"

This is Spirit Week at our school and today is Pajama Day:

Kid: Where are your pajamas, Mr. Gralen?

Me: I have to go pick up 750 pounds of clay in about an hour and I can't do that in my pajamas.

Kid: Why not?

Kid #1: I don't want to copy someone else's design.

Me: You're not copying, you're using it for inspiration. Besides, good artists copy, great artists steal. Steve Jobs said that, but he stole it from Picasso. Do you know who Picasso stole it from?

Kid #1: No.

Me: Stravinsky.

Kid #2: And Stravinsky stole it from my mom.

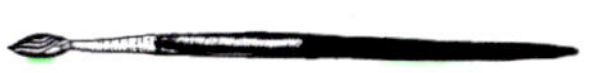

Kid: Mr. Gralen, you have to let us leave early for the ice cream social after school.

Me: That's not gonna happen. I have a legal responsibility for you up until the bell rings, and I actually take that pretty seriously.

Kid: We'll sign waivers.

Kid: I don't want to do it that way. You can't make me.

Me: Are you arguing with your parents a lot these days?

Kid: HOW DID YOU KNOW?

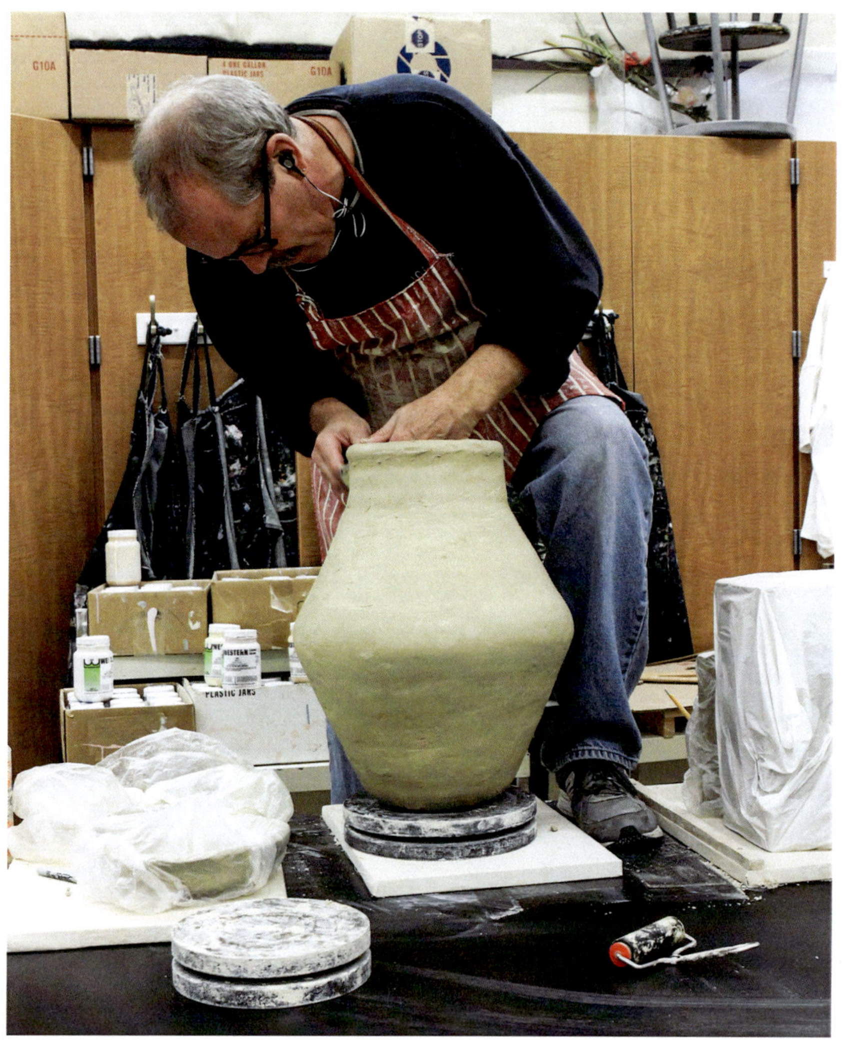

The Art Teacher At Work....

Kid: No one's gonna help me.

Me: That's a very passive aggressive way of saying you need some help.

Kid: That's how I roll.

Girl: Mr. Gralen, why are some boys so weird?

Me: Some of them are being weird because they are nervous because they really, really like you. When some boys are nervous they do weird things, and that's going to be the same for the rest of your life.

Girl: Ewwww.

Me: Do not throw things in here, do not toss things, do not fling things, do not hurl things, pitch things, lob things, or chuck things.

Kid: CHUCK NORRIS!

Me: Remember to save your file and upload it to Google drive, where it will be safe.

Kid: Supposedly.

52

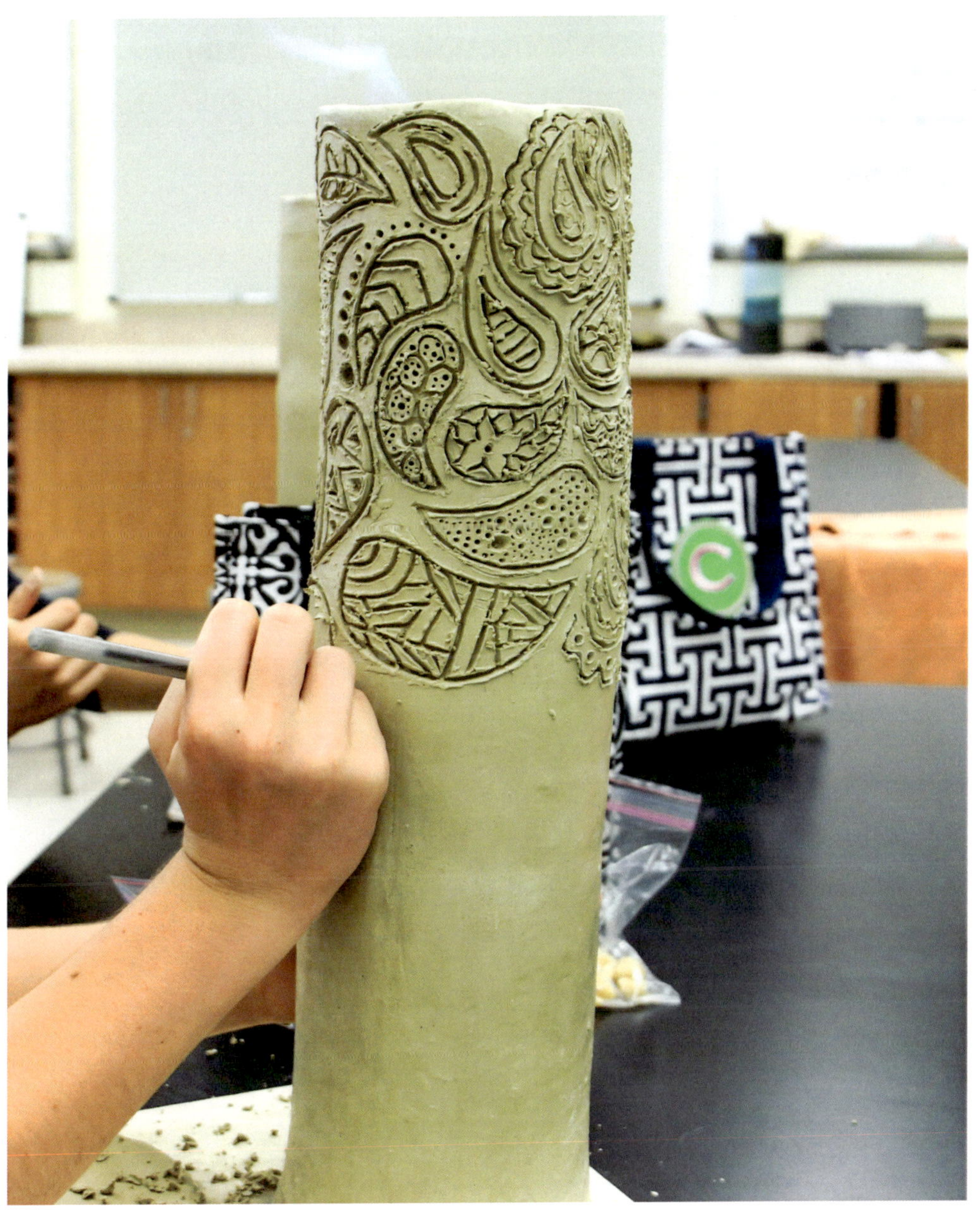

We are doing digital selfies in our 1A class and the kids get to choose a background image for a setting:

Me: You can choose where you want to be; for instance, maybe you'll choose a moonscape so you can be on the moon.

Kid: And……dead?

Me: There's a time and a place to swear, and our classroom is not the place nor the time. But it happens. Have you heard your parents swear?

Kid: Yeah, usually while parallel parking.

Kid: Mr. G., you know what's really annoying? When you think you know everything and you've got it all under control, and then two weeks later you're looking back and saying, "What was I doing with my life back then?"

Genius: "The hardest part was painting the sunflower petals, since they never turned out how I wanted them. However, I wasn't too upset about this, since sunflowers aren't perfect in real life."

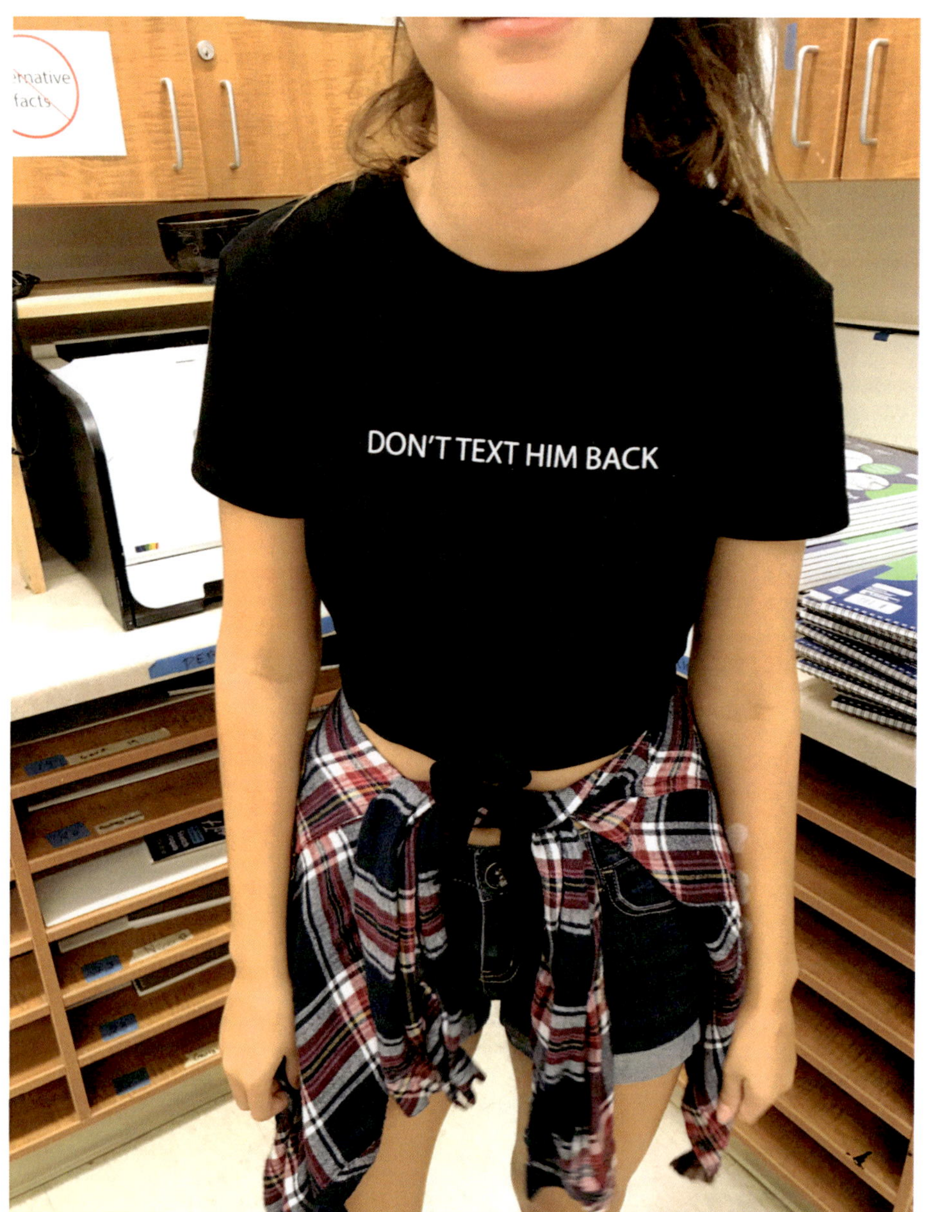

We are in the computer lab and I am playing Pandora – despite the "explicit lyrics" filter, something mildly inappropriate comes on:

Me: I'm going to be charged with corrupting you.

Kid: We're already corrupted.

Kid turns on computer, it doesn't boot instantly:

Kid#1: This computer does not work.

Me: Your inability to delay gratification is frightening.

Kid #2: What does that even mean? Are you an English teacher?

Kid #1: No, he's just got an art degree.

On teaching:…the job seems to require the sort of skills one would need to pilot a bus full of live chickens backwards, with no brakes, down a rocky road through the Andes while simultaneously providing colorful and informative commentary on the scenery.

-Franklin Habit

Kid: My dad wants to be a writer and photographer, that's such an old man dream. Every month he changes his old man dream.

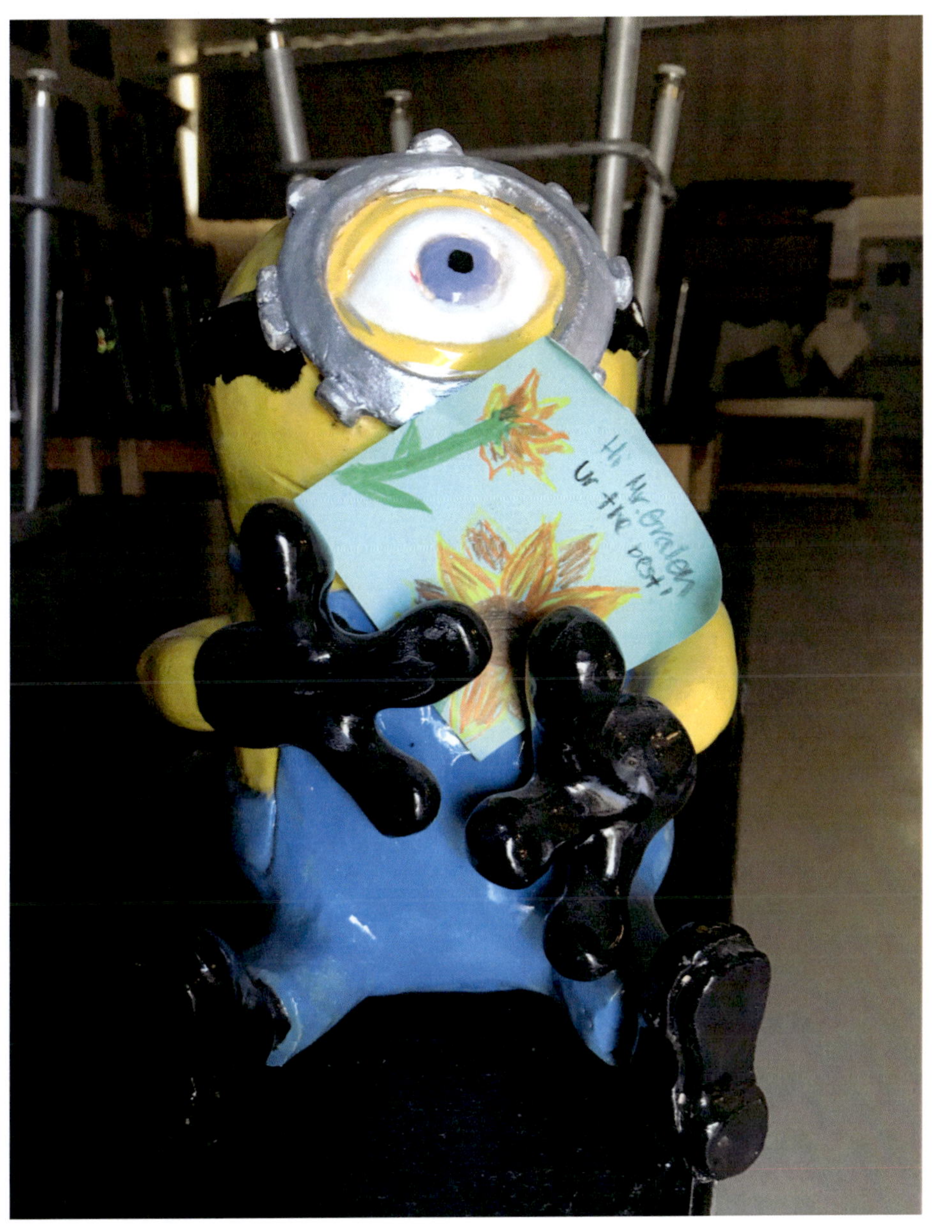

Me: Raise your hand and tell me one fun thing you did this weekend.

Kid: My entire family tried to play golf.

Me: What's wrong?

Kid: My stomach really hurts.

Me: What did you eat for breakfast this morning?

Kid: Coffee.

Kid: Mr. G., if they make the phone any bigger, they're going to need to come out with Apple Pants to make it fit.

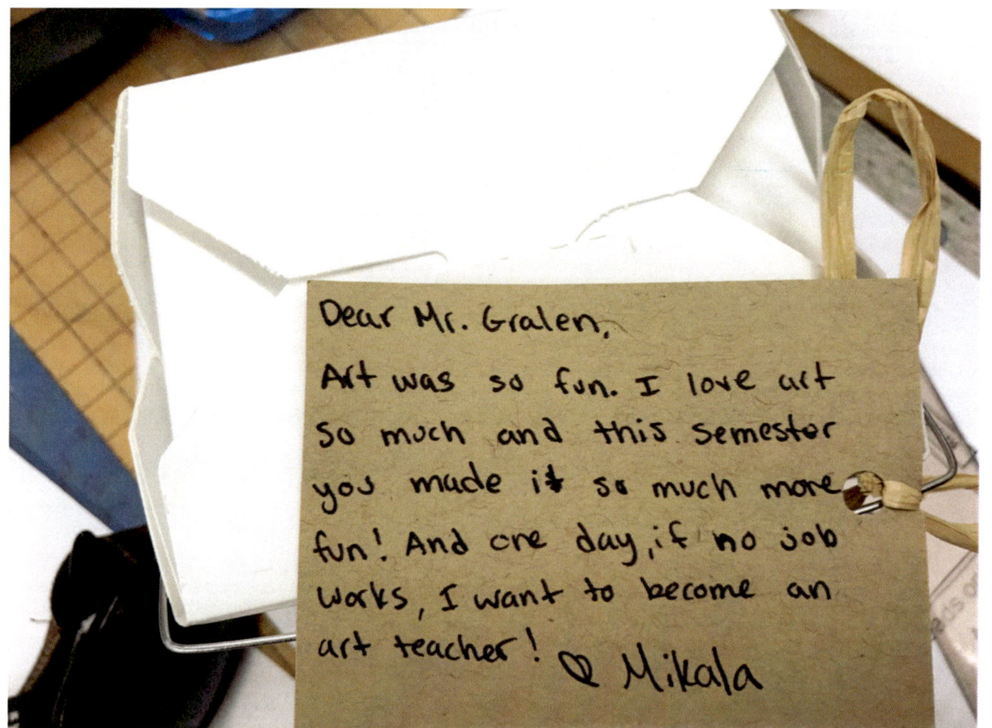

I like her back-up plan. It worked for me!

Kid: Mr. Gralen, how old were you when email was invented?

Me: Well, email has been around for a long time, but a lot of people started to use it in the mid-'90s, so I was about 35. Do you know anything about the history of the internet?

Kid: I know it was lame back then.

Kid is being hard on herself because she thinks everyone else is doing a better job on their drawing:

Me: The world is too crowded for you to be in competition with everyone else. The only person you need to be better than is the person you are right now.

Long pause….

Kid: Wow. You should be a motivational speaker.

Kid: You know what's really weird? When you feel really good when you buy a new iPhone and then a newer one comes out and you're like "Oh my god."

Kid: Money can't buy happiness, but it can buy books, and those are basically the same thing.

Me: Remember, I told you on Monday that your homework was to do something helpful at home without being asked.

Kid: I tried that and my mom got suspicious.

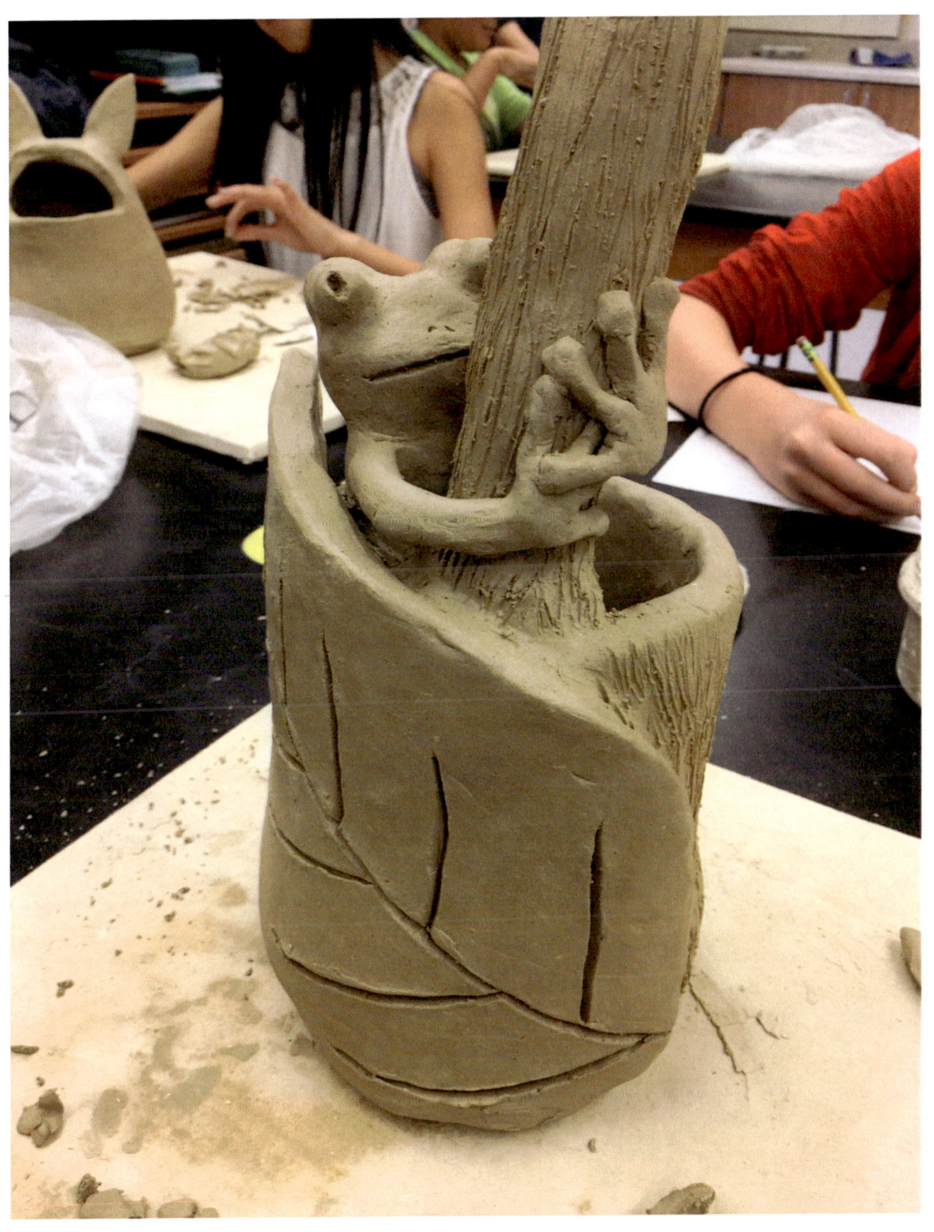

I had a student last year who is from Belgium. She came to see me today after spending the summer back home in Europe:

Me: Did you eat a lot of french fries with mayonnaise?

Kid: I've never understood that about Belgians. They do it all the time but they don't get fat like Americans.

I made a Lady Gaga station on Pandora:

Kid: Mr. Gralen, this playlist is not like your usual music.

Me: I'm trying to step outside of my comfort zone.

Kid: Thank God!

Playing the '80s stream, the first tune that comes on is Journey's "Don't Stop Believing". The kids went nuts. I facepalmed:

Me: You guys, this was a top hit the year I graduated from college.

Kid: Wait. My mom graduated from HIGH SCHOOL in 1980. That means…..

Long pause while I watch the gears turning…

Me: Yes. I'm older than your mom.

Kid: O_O

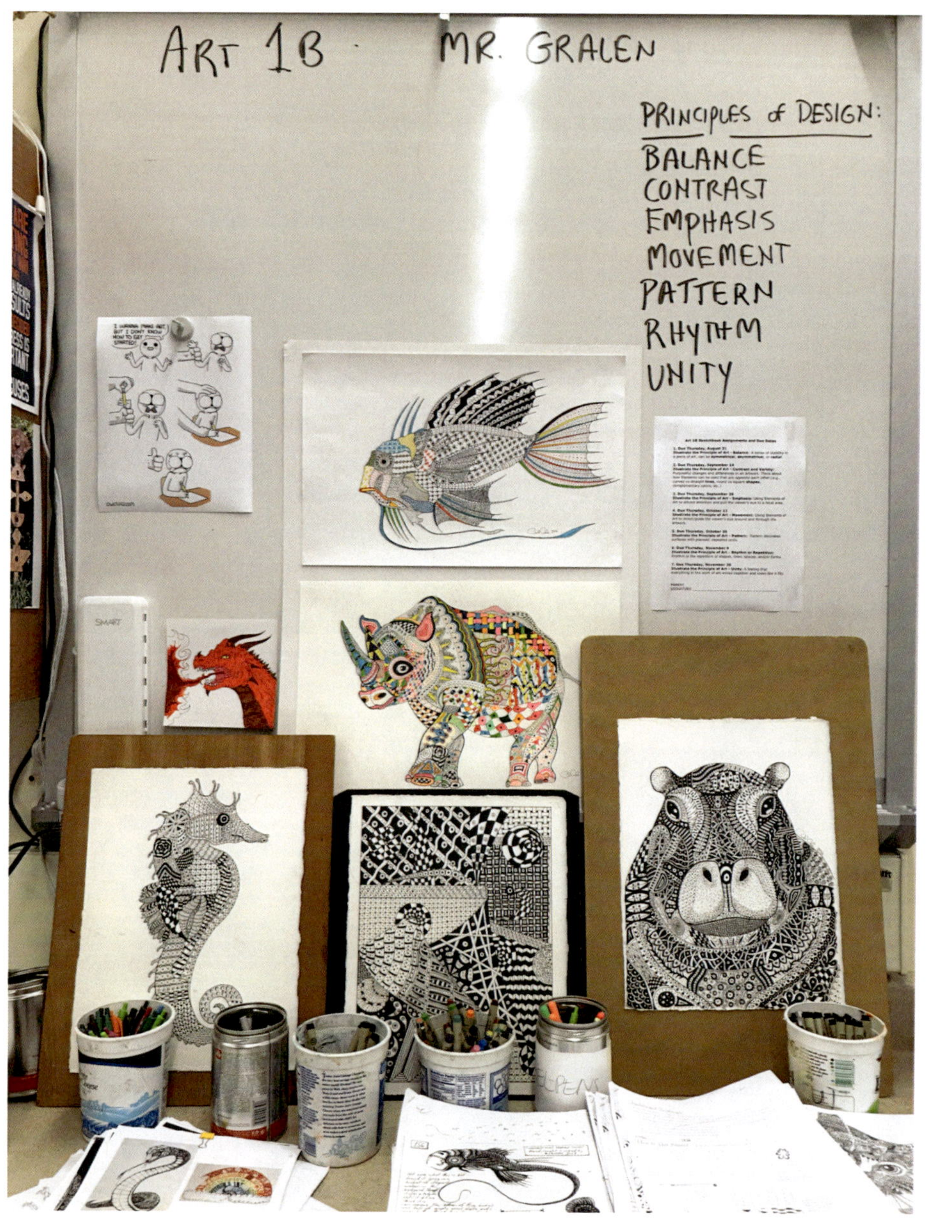

Me: Why are you late?

Kid: The bus broke down.

Me: You don't take a bus. You live three blocks away.

Kid: How do you know that?

Me: I know everything about stuff.

Kid: Mr. Gralen, you have to help me right now.

Me: You're an only child, aren't you?

Kid: Yeah, but how did you know that?

Kid: Wait, your mom let you use bourbon to get a stain out? That stuff's expensive!

Kid: Mr. G., where's my art award?

Me: Your award is my undying gratitude for your delightful presence in our classroom every morning.

Kid: That's not gonna cut it. I need cookies.

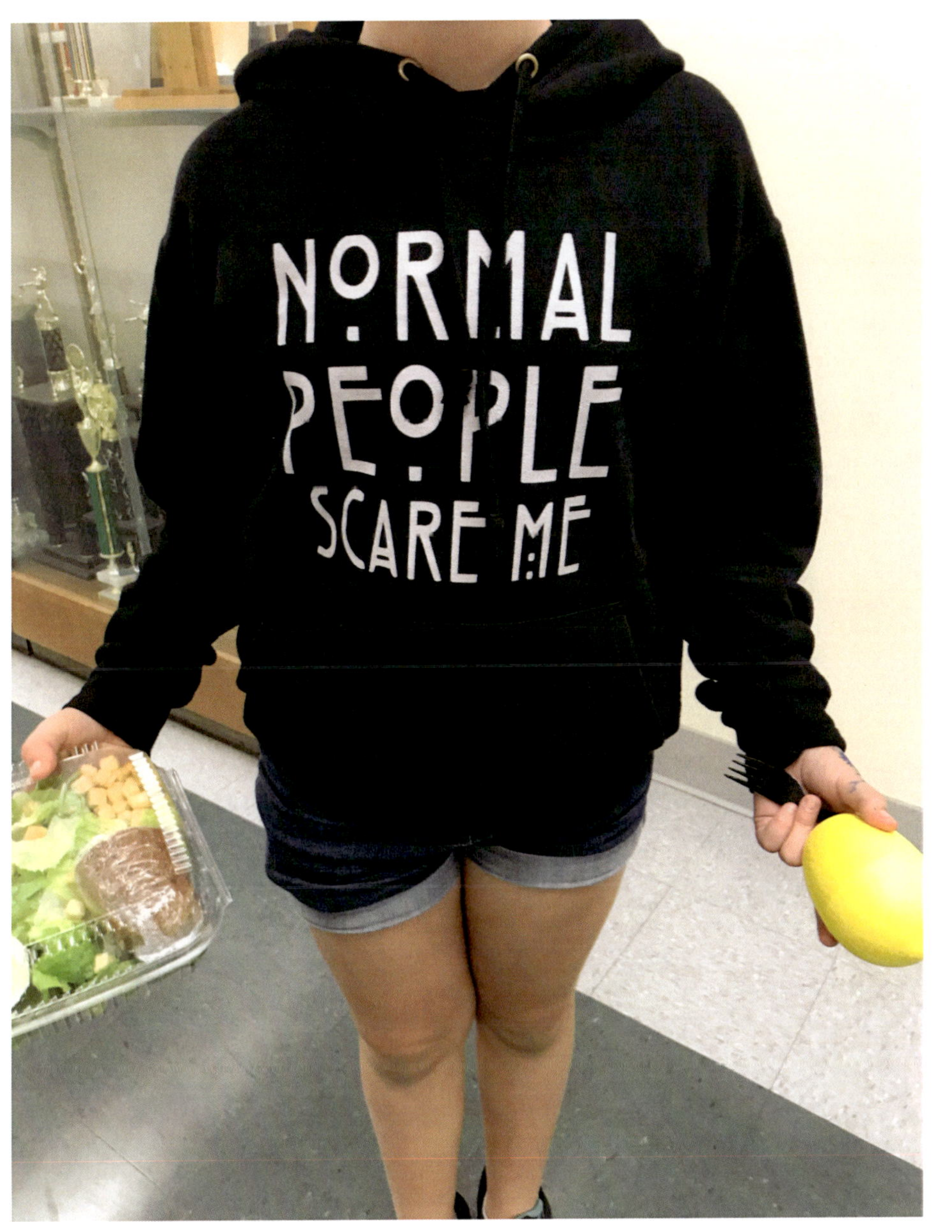

I showed my students a short video about mindfulness meditation, in which a kindergartner describes the brain as a jar of water full of glitter, all swirling around, and as you breathe, the glitter settles and you become calmer:

Kid: Mr. Gralen, our brains are not made of glitter. If they were, we'd all be dumb as bricks.

Me: I'm going to restrain myself here…..

It's only 8:20 a.m. and I've gotten the Quote of the Week already:

Kid: The year's gone by way too fast. I don't wanna go to high school.

Another Quote of the Week Award:

Kid: I'm so bummed. My mom wants me to go to this place next weekend and there's no WiFi.

I have my students do a short "artist's statement" about their mask project:

Kid: My mask represents how people hide behind a beautiful mask to conceal who they really are. They pretend to be their idea of a perfect human being which does not exist. I made this mask to show how if you remove your outer mask then people will learn about the real you.

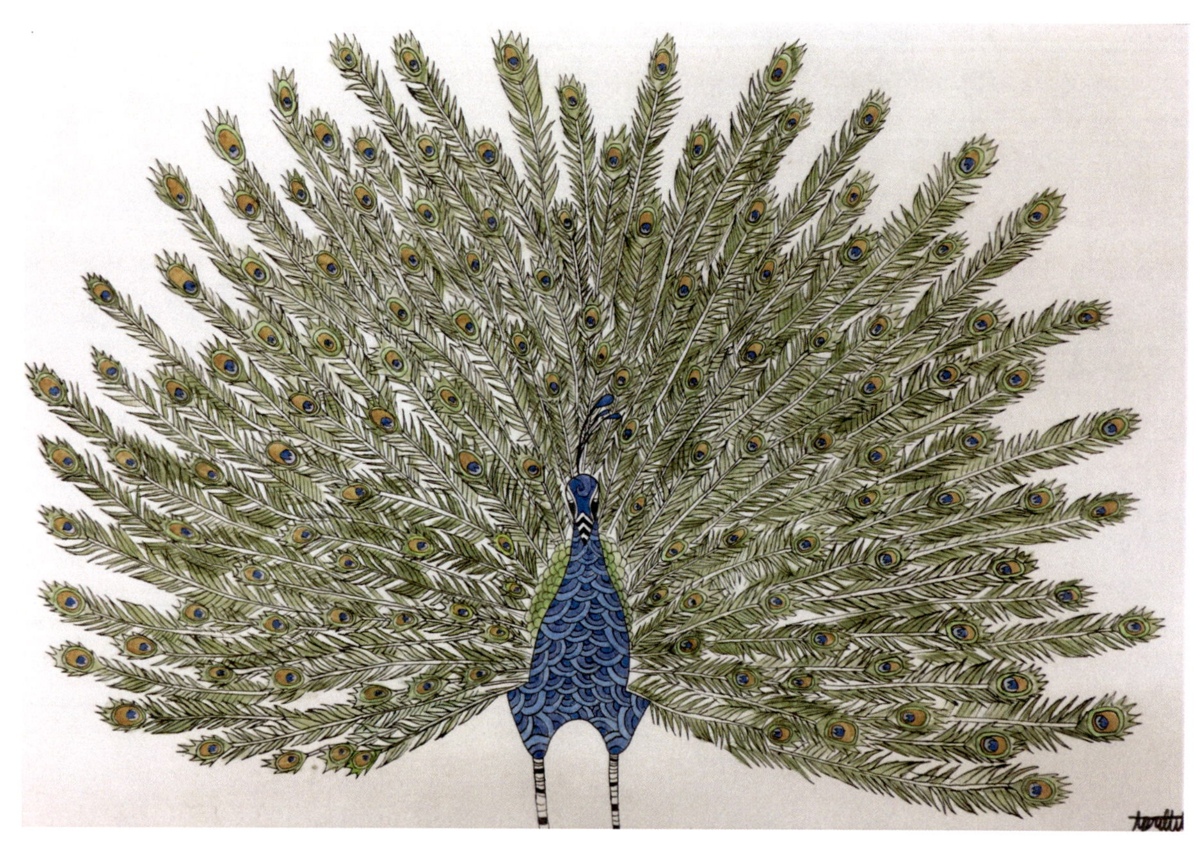

One of my favorite, most mischievous students showed up this morning with a broken arm. I asked him what happened and so far
I have received 5 versions:

My parachute didn't open all the way.
I got bitten by a shark.
I was curling about 100 pounds and it broke.
I lost the sumo match.
My little sister hit me."

Will add to the list as it gets longer…..

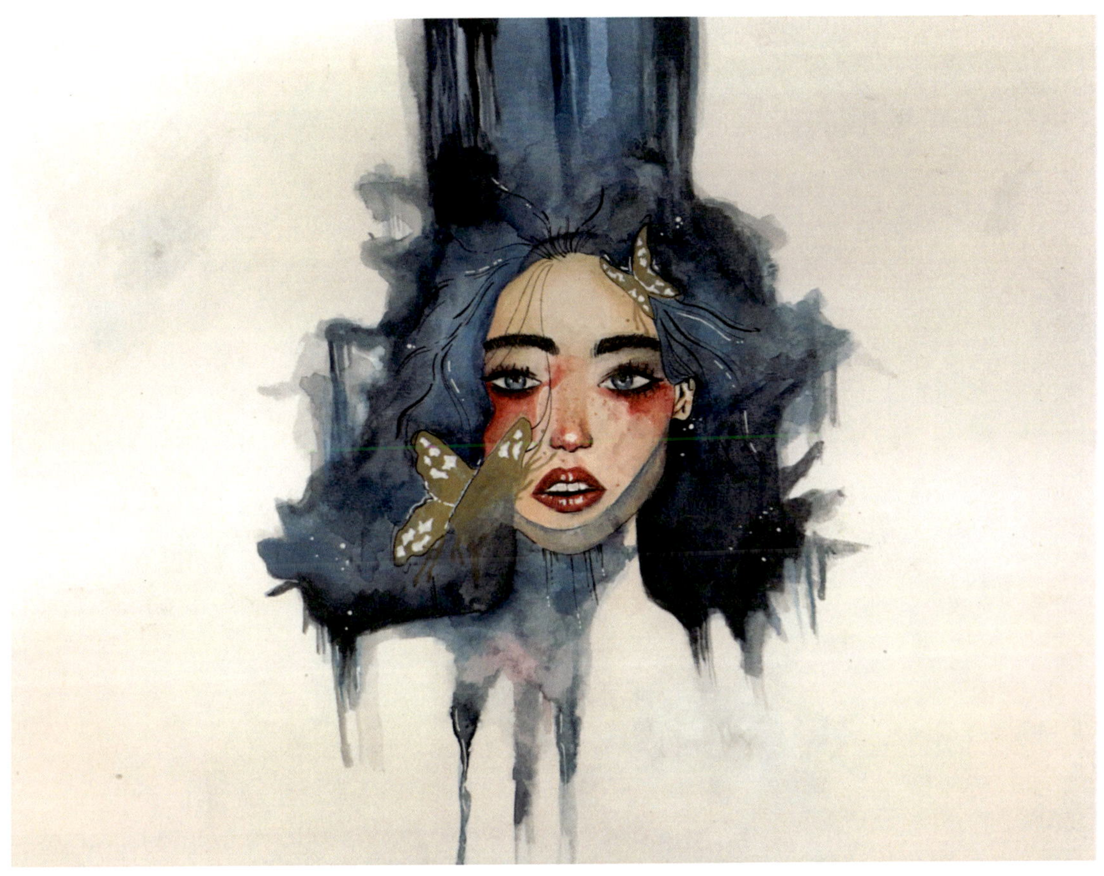

Kid #1: Mr. G., here's a question: you have the clothes on your back and a knife. You can take one thing with you to survive in the harsh wilderness. What do you take with you?

Me: I'd take a flint and a striker so I could make fire.

Kid #2: I'd take a helicopter.

Me: Are you arguing with your parents a lot these days?

Kid: Let's just say we've agreed to disagree.

Quote of the day:

Kid: I really don't want to use earthworms in my design because they're weird. You can't tell which way they're going.

Kid: I've decided to get a tattoo.

Me: You'll want to think long and hard about that, and then make the decision when you are a fully grown adult with a clear head.

Kid: But that gives me way too much time – then I'll never be able to make a bad decision.

I make my Ceramics students destroy the first pinch pot they make because it's just practice and they will make more and better ones as they go along. Plus it's just clay:|

Kid: Starting over would be like dying and having to re-live your entire life all over again from the very beginning.

I can see I have my work cut out for me.

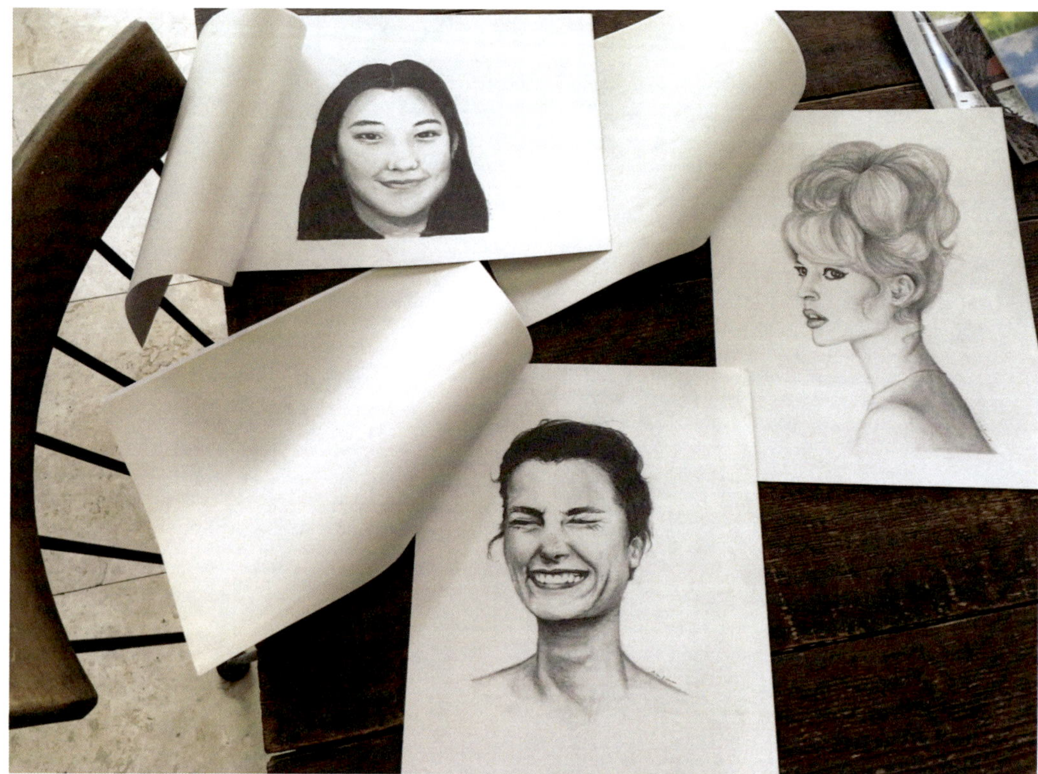

Pencil drawings by a very talented 8th-grader.

I was trying to give some gentle advice to a kid regarding the design for his Op Art project, which was quite ambitious and based on the radial balance symmetry of a turbine engine. I was pointing out something that could be a stumbling block in his geometry and he looked at me like I was an idiot:

Kid: "I'm fully aware of that, but recursively it will all work out in the long run."

I love my job.

Kid#1: Mr. Gralen, why do they call it "tardy"?

Kid #2: Well, in Spanish "tarde" means "late".

Kid #1: But we're in America!

Kid: That guy in "American Sniper" died the most ironic death ever.

Other kid: I don't know. Elvis died on the toilet.

Kid comes into my room at 8 a.m. dressed in shorts and a t-shirt. It's about 45 degrees outside. He is shivering like a leaf in the wind:

Me: Dude, you're cold because you aren't dressed properly. You need a jacket and long pants.

Kid: That's exactly what my mom said to me this morning.

Me: Well, why don't you listen to her?

Kid: Because I can't let her win.

Kid: You know how some kids have the "terrible twos"? My sister's had that her whole life.

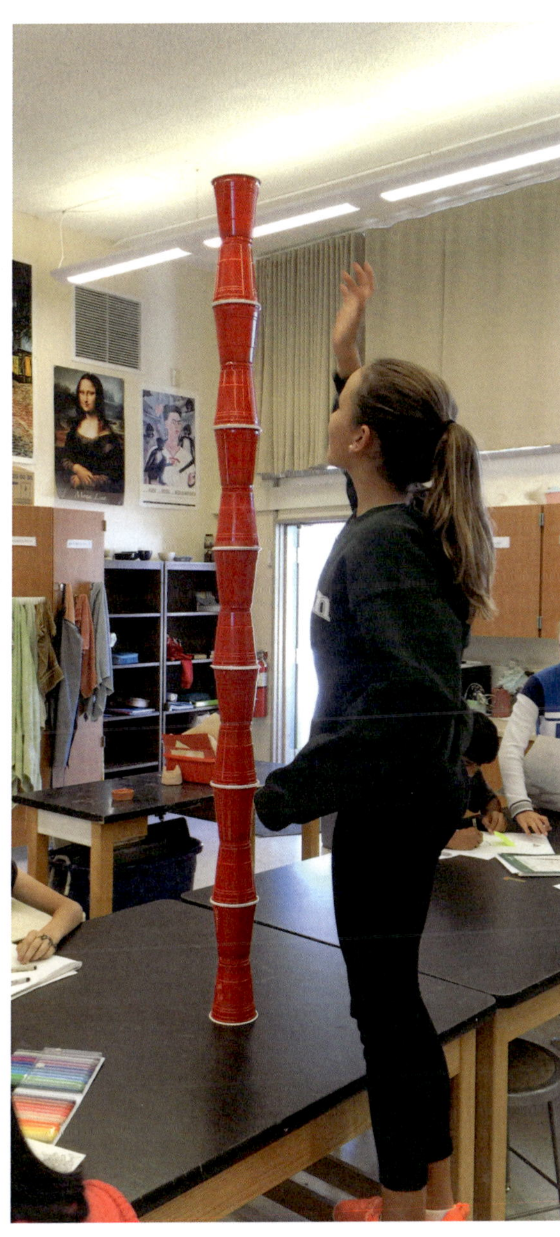

Kid: No, no, no, she's not a psychopath, she's a sociopath. There's a difference.

Kid: No, don't do it that way, you'll make his knuckles bleed.

Me: No making each other bleed, that's not OK.

Kid: What about internally?

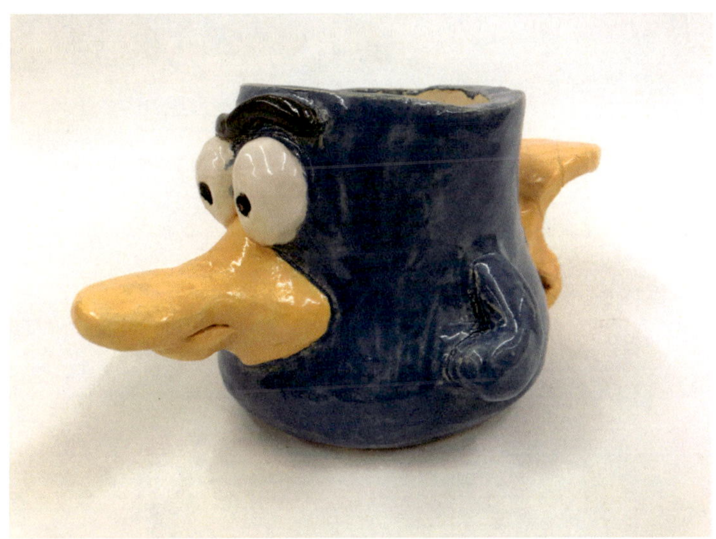

Killing time before the bell…

63

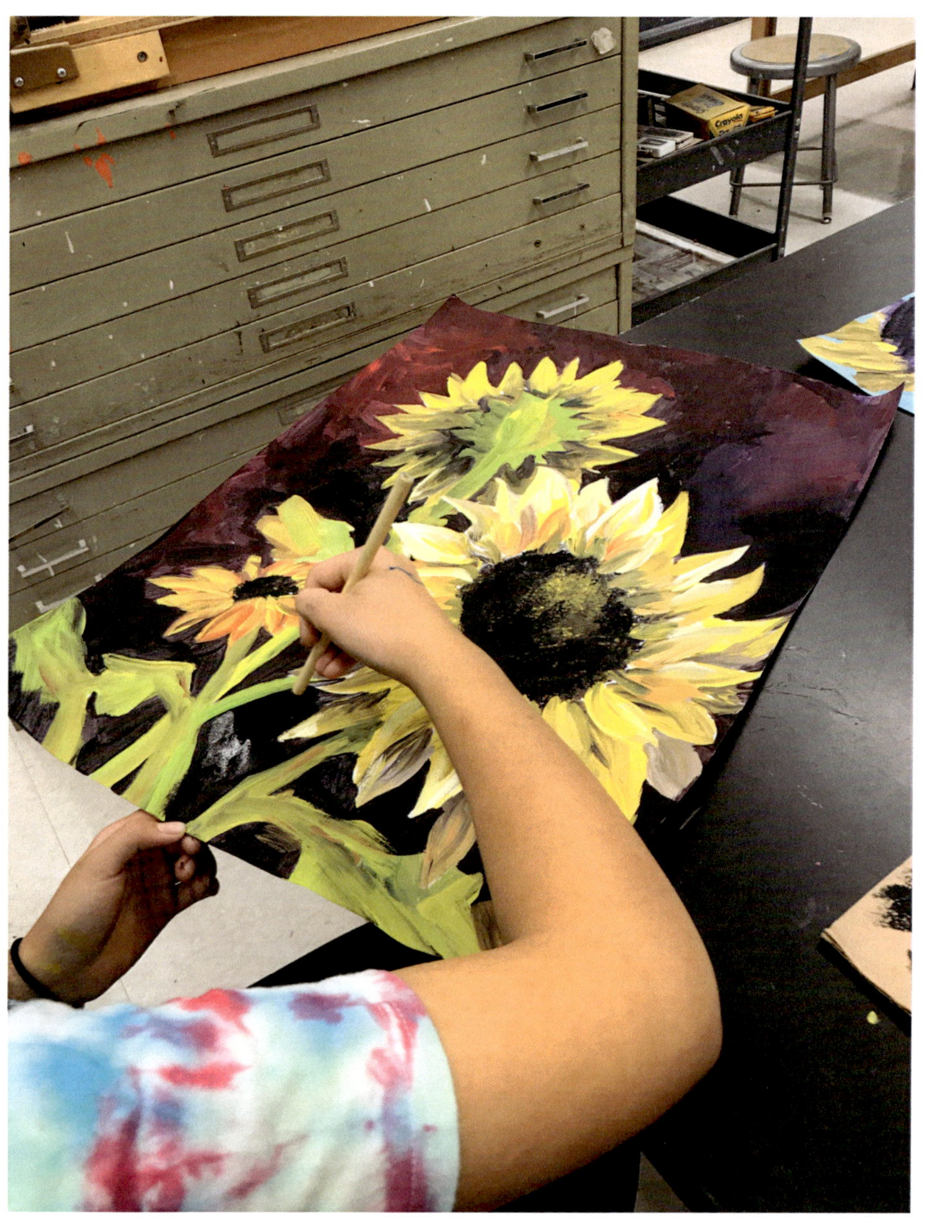

Quote of the day:

Kid: Maurice, you're smart. Is it OK to eat expired macarons?

Me: This pen set is a total mess. Why do you guys do this to me?

Kid: I have OCD, I will totally sort that out for you.

Kid #1: Why is this piece so bad?

Me: How many times have you done this?

Kid #1: Once.

Me: When you do it for the 30th time, do you think it will be better?

Kid #1: Mr. Gralen, is this art class, or that other thing, what do you call it, what was it that guy Socrates did?

Kid #2: Philosopher.

Kid #1: Yeah. This feels more like a philosophy class when you say stuff like that.

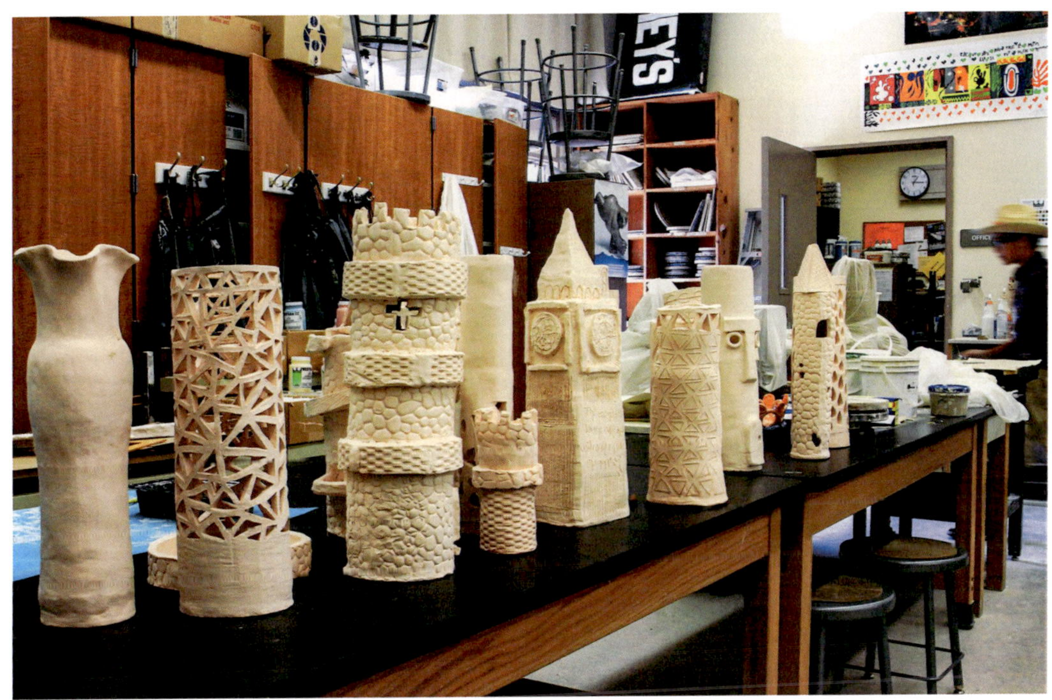

Kid: I am really happy with my sculpture.

Me: That's great. Happy students are one of our goals.

Kid: Do you get paid more if we're happy?

Wisdom from the middle school classroom, episode 12:

If life gives you lemons, you really can't make lemonade unless life gives you some sugar to work with too.

Talking to my Ceramics class:

Me: I showed the PTA your work today and they were really impressed and gave me a bunch of money.

Kid: I think we deserve at least 15% of that.

Teacher moment of the day:

Kid: Mr. Gralen, how do you spell "thermometer"?

Me: Let's sound it out – you've got "thermo" and then "meter". Which means "to measure temperature" – "thermo" is a root for "heat" and "meter" is a root for "measuring".

Kid: Is that how they figured it out? That's so cool! It's not completely nonsensical!

Kid: I'm done with my sculpture.

Me: What can you do at this point to refine and improve your work?

Kid: I'm going to give it a tramp stamp.

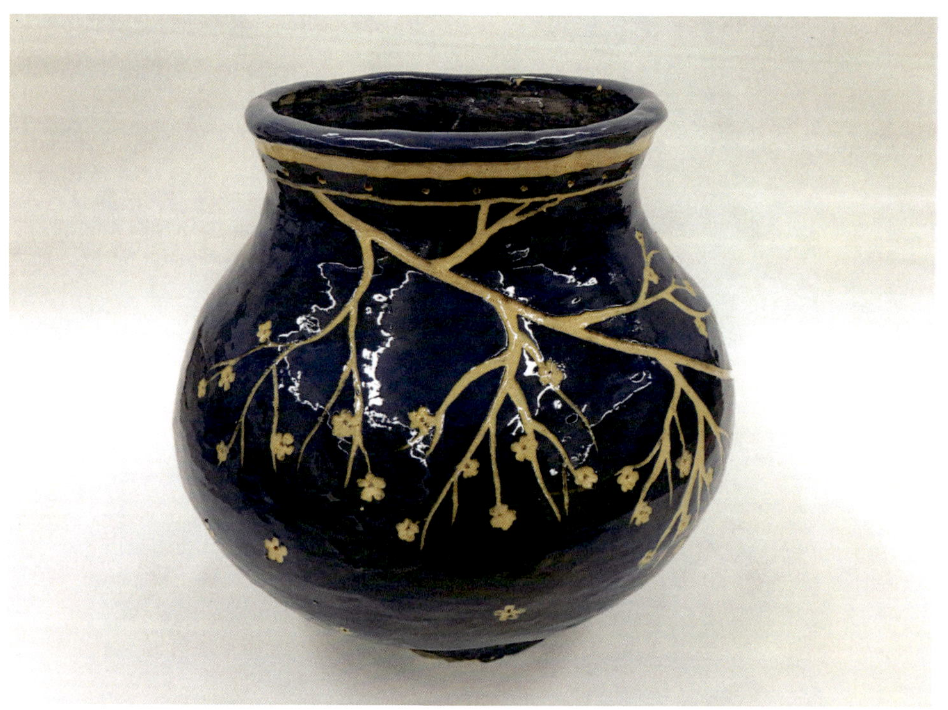

The lesson was on self-portraits, and I was talking about how important it was to be honest about how we looked:

Me: If I'm going to be honest, I have to admit that I've gained about 25 pounds in the last ten years.

Super-wise 8th grade girl: Well, if I'm going to be honest, Mr. G., I have to admit that I've gained over 100 pounds in the last ten years….

Quote of the week:

Kid: I wanna go live in a cabin in the woods and hang out with Hunter Pence and read novels and eat squirrel meat. And venison.

Wishing my kids well over Spring Break:

Me: OK you guys, have fun, be safe, hold hands, and look both ways when you cross the street.

Kid: But if you hold hands both people die because it's harder to run.

Me: How much sugar did you have at lunch?

Kid: Not much. I have a natural energy because of my youth.

Me: You guys need to do a better job of cleaning up after yourselves. The maid quit last week.

Kid in back of room: Wait, we had a maid?

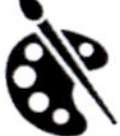

Kid: Mr G., you act like a kid a lot. But in a good way.

Me: Well, my wife says I dress like a twelve year-old.

Kid: Well, you sort of do. That hoodie, for instance. I'd get rid of that if I were you.

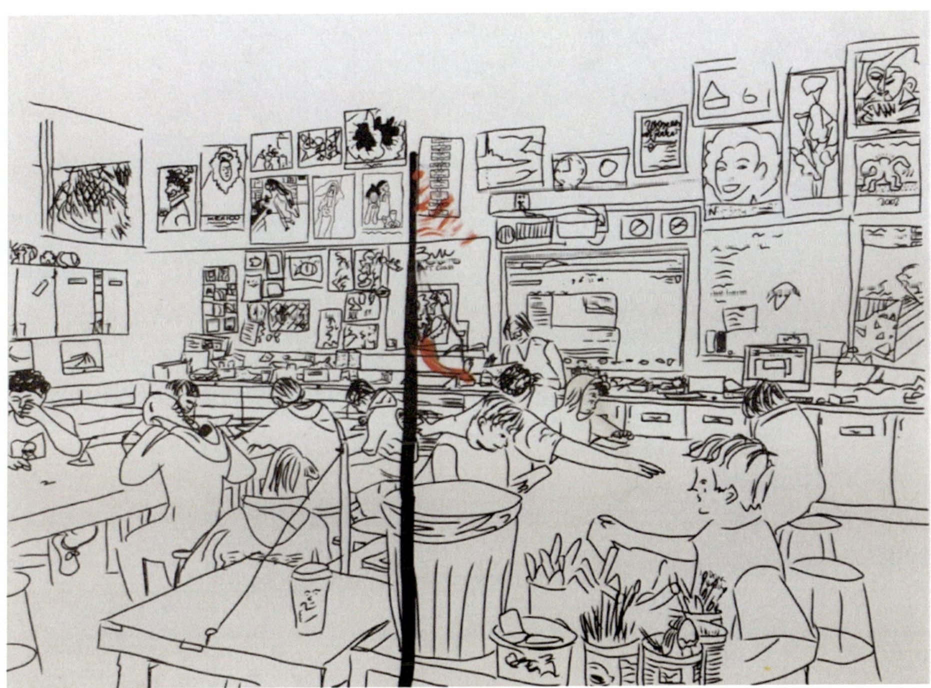

Kid #1 is working with incredible precision on a clay project:

Me: It's your perfectionist side coming out.

Kid #2: Is she being fussy again?

Me: Well, it's good training for when she becomes a dentist or a surgeon. You want her to be fussy when she's working on your tooth.

Kid #2: Or your brain.

Kid #3: Or your right buttock.

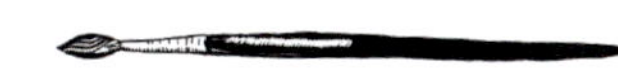

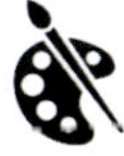

New 8th grade girl strategy:

Kid: My mom is so paranoid – if I'm going to meet a boy, I just say to her, "It's OK, Mom, he's gay."

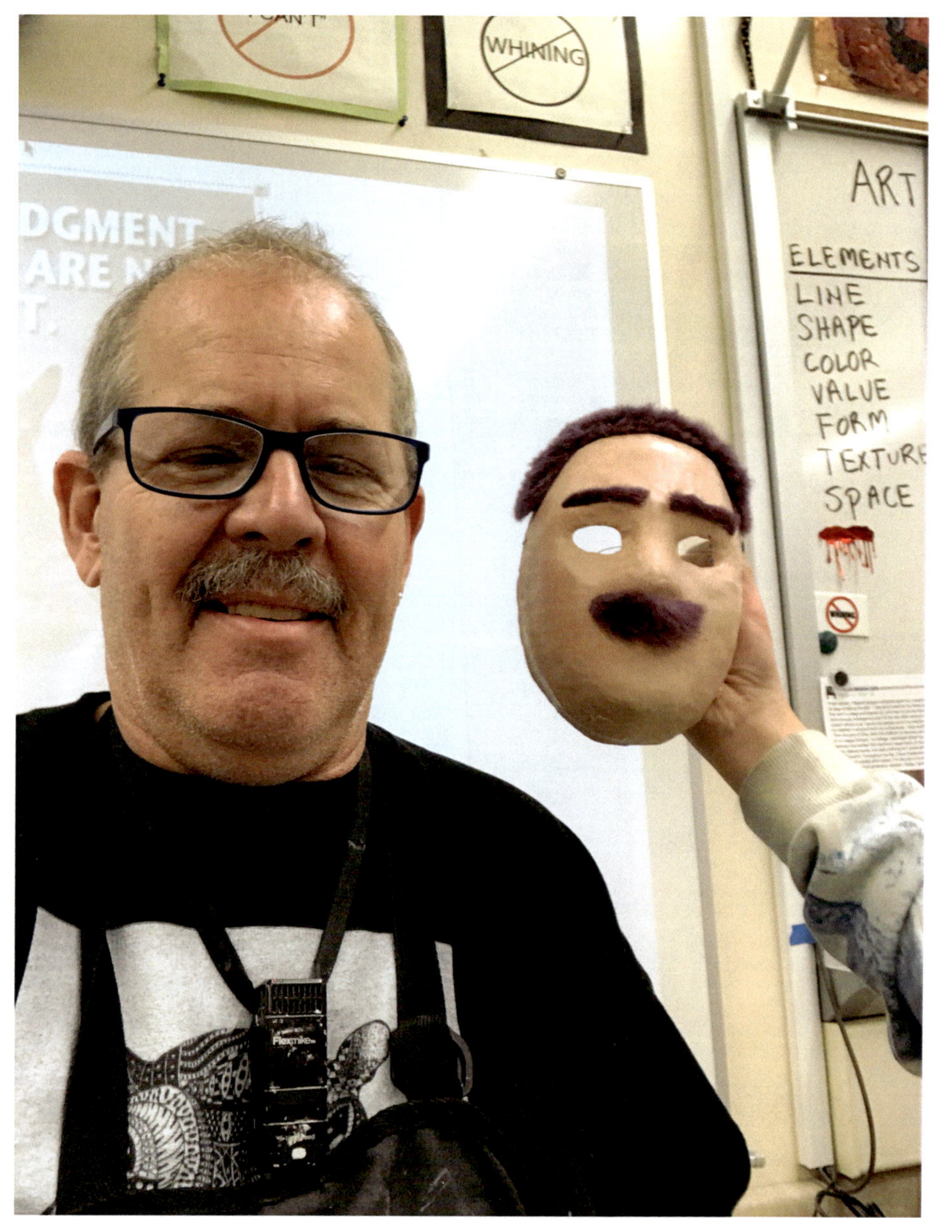

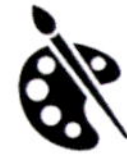

The discipline of most of the students I am paid to teach is deplorable. They claim to forget their assignments, when in truth, they simply refused to do them. They do not want to learn, and I cannot instill that desire in them. Our nation is doomed. - Aristotle

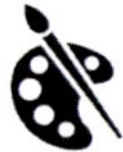

The 14-year old girl sitting in front of me on the stage at graduation last night is being humorously teased by the 13-year old boys on either side of her:

Girl: Mr. Gralen, they're being so stupid, make them stop.

Me: You realize this is a situation that's never going to change, right?

Girl: *Sigh* Mr. Gralen, you're killin' me here.

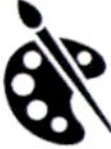

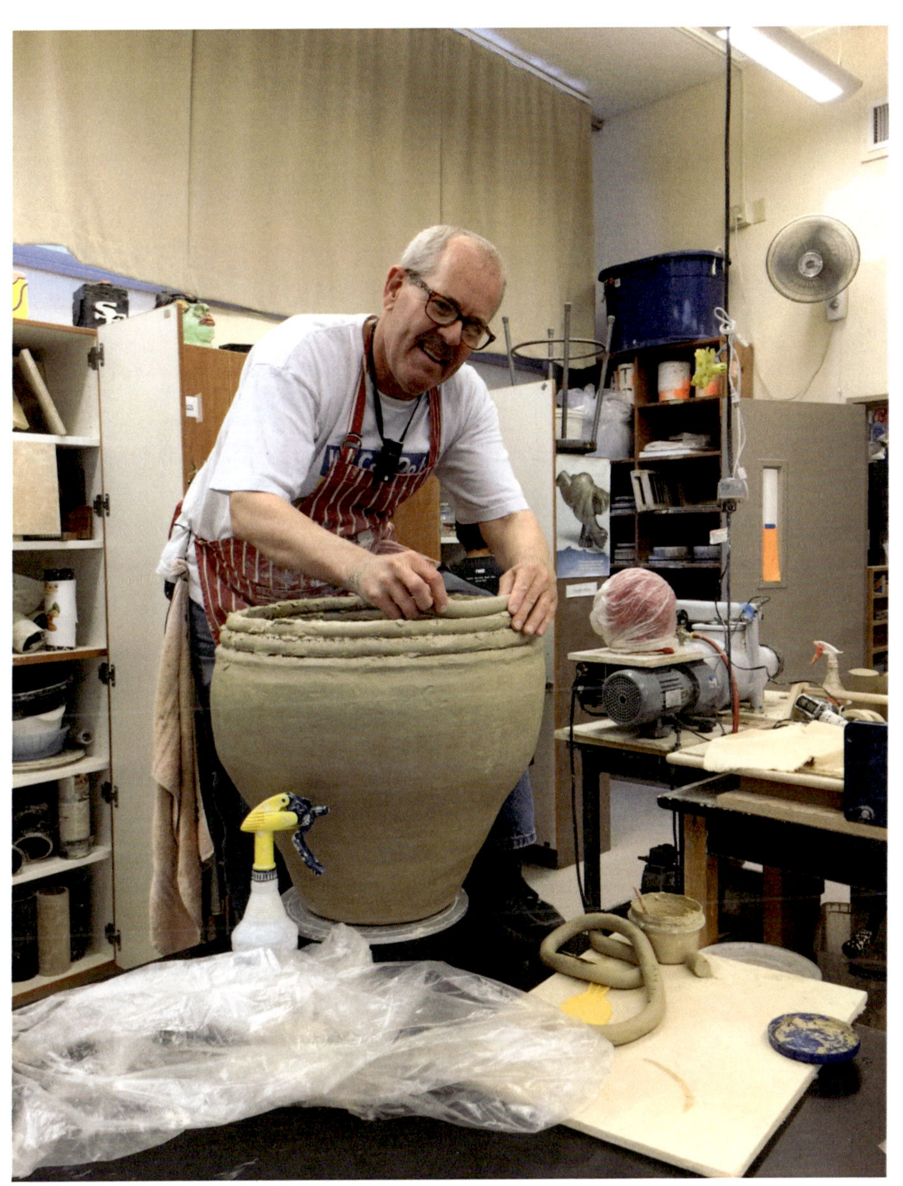

I did not set out to become an art teacher. If you had told me twenty-five years go that I would end up teaching art to middle schoolers in the middle of Silicon Valley, I would have said you were nuts. But that's what happened, and I could not have asked for a better continuous lesson in magic, beauty, humility, the power of creativity, the joy of learning, and a constant daily reminder that you just never know what the next moment is going to bring.

There were days that were immensely challenging.

And then there were days when the magic of creativity flowed as if coming from an unending fountain of joy at the heart of the universe. In the end, I would not have traded it for anything.

–PG

9 7982 18 252311